SPIRITUAL PHENOMENA
AND
WALK IN SOULS

BY
LINDA COWLEY WILKS
"LOVELY"

Spiritual Phenomena and Walk In Souls
ISBN: 978-1-73262-620-1

DEDICATION

This book is dedicated to my charming daughter Shatira Wilks-Smelser who's love and dedication has inspired many to seek the best within themselves, including me. Her kind loving spirit soars to the heights where Angels abide.

Thank you Shatira for publishing my book and helping my dream of becoming an Author, a reality for all to enjoy.

CONTENTS

I OFFER DEEP GRATITUDE

TO MY SPIRIT GUIDES FOR

THEIR IMMENSE WISDOM AND

THE PREPARATION

OF THIS BOOK

ACKNOWLEDGMENTS

My first love, my father Nolen Cowley who directed me towards the way of spirit through words and deeds while his actions offered me sight and direction to walk the path of spirit. He demonstrated his ability to love as he walked with me on the path of light until I could stand on my own. Although he has made his transition, I often feel the presence of his love and wisdom   .

My lovely daughter Shatira Wilks, for her unceasing love and support. Thanks for believing in me and sharing your insight into the creation and publishing of this book. The patience and joy that she has provided on my journey has propelled me forward, as she nudged me constantly to finish this book.

Kofi Maalik Ph.d. I offer appreciation for your friendship. Your immediate recognition of the soul exchange caused me to understand the soul transference that had taken place. The offering of a listening ear and viable information has assisted me from the beginning of the soul exchange to the finishing of this book. Thanks for offering me an understanding of a walk in soul as well as a historical accounts.

Norrie Amoako, student of the Ascended Masters Instruction. Thanks for your diligent support and information regarding the Ascended Masters. The teachings and instruction has been a valuable asset. Your assistance and foresight offered light upon this journey.

June May Kortum, Medium. Founder and Executive Director of The Gathering Lighthouse. Thank you for providing a platform where I was given an opportunity to express my true essence without judgement. Your support and enthusiasm provided the light for me to bare my soul.

Renee Lenore Oswald, CHt, RMP, CGLT, thanks for believing in me. Your confidence and support created the path to the writing of this book. My appreciation for you is constant.

Bakarie Wilks II, thanks for being the first to lay eyes upon my manuscript. Your feedback was enthralling. Your continuous love and support is to be cherished as well as your technical insights.

James Smelser, thanks for your technical support and relentless belief in this book. Your steadfast support in so many ways are worthy of my gratitude.

Gwendolyn Johnson, I hold deep gratitude for all that you offered in the production of this book.

Those who have played a role in propelling me forward, through inspiration, support and belief in me are too many to mention. I offer a deep genuine appreciation for your presence on my spiritual journey.
Love and Light

FOR BOOKINGS,

SPEAKING ENGAGEMENTS,

TELEVISION, RADIO, & PRINT

MEDIA, ETC...

CONTACT:

LINDA COWLEY WILKS

www.youcanbooklinda.com

youcanbooklinda@gmail.com

OR

SHATIRA WILKS

shatirawilks@gmail.com

FORWARD

I AM writing this book with the desire and hope that it becomes an open door that humanity may peek within the corridors of the spiritual world and step into rooms that may not have been explored. To gain entry one must release the fears that have hindered their journey into the world of spirit, where all matters of life and death reside. All other aspects of life fit neatly in between these two powerful expressions of the spirit. A peek into the unknown can be a potent seed planted into the minds of the people here on planet earth. The information provided can open the eyes of the masses that they may become more enlightened regarding the functions and powers held within the souls of mankind. Understanding all aspects and powers of the spirit will continuously be elusive. Those who seek spiritual insight understand that the road is wide and infinite, yet it brings joy to the traveler. The physical body encases the spirit yet the power that it wields has not been exposed to the masses. The door has been cracked open, for those willing to step in and honor the true essence of who they are. Society is yearning for a sense of truth. Within these pages truth can be discovered. While the well is deeper than the imagination, we must continue to partake of it's waters of wisdom. Those who choose to read this book will find a cup filled to the brim with wisdom, knowledge and informa-

My father was determined to keep my brother and I intact and with him as he took a strong stand with those who wanted to rear his children. A grandmother and several aunts attempted to convince my father that the children would be better off under their care. He was steadfast in keeping my brother and I with him.

After several years my father remarried. I had a stepmother who was not kind and often told me that she did not know how to love me. Yet she kept my brother and I in a Christian Church that offered the beginning of my spiritual foundation. I am thankful for the foundation. It became a spring-board for my spiritual journey. I now understand that she had never felt love, therefore she did not know how to love. She claimed to have had two mean stepmothers. She modeled herself after them.

Navigating through my teen years was not an easy task. I was anx-ious to turn eighteen years old to gain control of my life on my own and to exit my parents home. My love for books had increased during this time of my life. While my father purchased my first car at the age of fifteen I gained more freedom.

I convinced by best friend, who I'll call Tam to ride with me to a neighboring state to pick up a particular book in regards to King Solomon. We were to ride in secret to ensure that our parents would not be aware of such a drive that would not be approved of. With our strategic planning, we were discovered due to me being involved in a fender bender where my friend Tam's leg was injured. This was a costly lesson to learn.

While sitting on the grounds of my high school with a friend, who has now made her transition, her uncle who was older had a deep interest in me. I knew nothing of male, female relationships. Having more experience than me since he had been in the military as well as had been married, his influence was evident. It felt like a whirlwind, pregnancy then marriage.

During this marriage I learned how to delve into the opposite of good.The marriage didn't work out. Until lately I still celebrated my divorce from my ex-husband. I have been divorced so long that the celebrations should have ceased many years ago. Yet I continued to celebrate the day that my divorce was finalized.

It was a very stressful marriage yet the marriage produced two of the most beautiful children on planet earth. At least that's what I thought at the time. The stress of the marriage and divorce eroded on my parenting skills. How good could the parenting skills of an 18-year-old be after all. After traveling what seems for ever in the dark tunnel of divorce court, I firmly made a decision that I would never marry again. I knew that my life had to change and it had to start with me. I needed to work on my emotions in order to develop and maintain a healthy relationship with myself as well as the opposite sex.

I was not aware at the time, but I had become a bag lady. A bag lady is considered to be a woman who carries past anger, hurt and resentment from an old relationship into new relationships. A so-called bag lady unconsciously diminishes the value of a new relationship. Whatever our dominate feelings are we carry within us everywhere we go. A new mate is generally the recipient of the anger and resentment that should have been resolved and left in the old relationship. As I look back I was more than a regular bag lady. I was a super duper bag lady. I balanced those bags like a ballerina as I danced through life unaware of the dark emotional weight that I was carrying.

How well I learned to become an emotional and verbal abuser. The dark memories of that marriage flowed through my life for a long period of time. As I reflected back I thought that marriage should never be permitted for an 18 year old. I attempted to rid myself of the heavy emotions that I carried. I finally acknowledged that I had to change the way that I looked at my ex husband. I had to consider him as a teacher on my journey through life. All teachers would not be gentle loving and kind as we humans would like to think. I saw him as one of my harshest teachers, yet there are deep profound lessons that one can learn.

Harsh lessons impact us deeply and if we learn we never have to repeat the lessons again. An important aspect was that I learned to forgive. A powerful lesson indeed. Without him crossing my path I may have never considered the forgiveness factor.

I discovered that forgiveness would unshackle every aspect of my being, mind, body, and spirit. Over time emotional balance and harmony were restored.

CHAPTER 1

RETRIEVING EMOTIONAL
AND SPIRITUAL
FREEDOM

Once I uprooted the old emotional debris, I began to look at the past exactly as I should, as non-existent, a situation that has gone on that cannot and should not be carried into my future. This revelation occurred much later in life. A sense of lightness permeated me as this idea took root. Periodically I would cross paths with my ex-husband. Instead of playing the blame game, by looking outward at him, I would monitor my feelings and look inward at me. Finally I arrived at a place where I no longer felt the sting of resentment. I knew that I was free.

During the course of my life I began to seek deeper spiritual understanding from different religious points of view. Organized religion was nothing new to me. I grew up in an average Christian based church, yet I knew there was more to God than was being taught.

Reading was very important to me. As a child a gift of a book was of great value. I never can remember a time when I did not love books. My love for reading stemmed from inquisition rather than entertainment. I was always drawn to books that captivated my attention. Books that filled my mind with wonder, intrigue and left me asking more questions. Much of my spare time was spent reading books that stimulated my curiosity. Books relevant to spirituality, psychology, astrology and a variety of religions where constant.

There was never a time that I didn't have a deep love for God. God and books went hand in hand. I thought that the creator belonged strictly to me. Every book that I read would give me more insight into the physical, mental and spiritual aspects of humans. Books that revealed the deeper meanings of life seemed to be drawn to me.

I began to notice that as I would grow spiritually into the next step of my spiritual journey, a teacher truly awaited me. I began to see the true meaning of a wise one who once said " when the student is ready the teacher will appear". Often the teacher was a human and other times it was a book, pamphlet, a symbol or an odd and unusual encounter. Something was always teaching me.

There were times that my dreams became my teacher. This may seem far-fetched to many. Those who hold these gifts and have had these experiences will attest to the validity of these words. Dreams can offer insight into solving problematic situations that one may be faced with. Some dreams offer information regarding future events. There is deep value in the dream state.

It has been proven and demonstrated through the sciences that all humans dream. It is considered the REM state. Many claim to not remember their dreams. Not remembering ones dreams is not an indicator that you do not dream. The dream world became an important aspect of my life.

There was a time in my life that I believed that everyone identified with the dream world as a system of communications that simply poured forth from another place. I paid strict attention to my dreams as my father coached me to do so at a very young age.

As I became more aware of the importance of taking care of the body, the mind and the spirit, my reading intensified and I began to learn the ways and means towards good health. Somehow over the years I expand- ed my knowledge of different health modalities. I began to detest toxins and harmful chemicals. I became more aware of my eating habits. Of course different types of health issues were presented in my studies as well as miraculous healings.

I began to draw those who embraced good health into my circle of associates and friends. Some became my teachers. I gained a deeper respect for all religions. I made a firm decision to extract what I determined to be in alignment with my beliefs and incorporate them into my life. I began to expand my awareness as to who or what God meant to me. Reading was generally the first thing that I did in the morning and the very last thing that I did at night. My thirst for knowledge has not waned in the least.

This is a part of me that many have not known. It seems that society wants to look at the outer form of a person, do a visual eye sweep, then

4

quickly claim that they know who you are, what you are made of as well as your futuristic possibilities. I was one who was very mindful of my mind, body and spirit connection. The majority of the time in my awareness I kept an invisible guard at the door of my mind. I felt in this manner the thoughts that would penetrate or affect me emotionally would only be the ones that I welcomed; thoughts of a higher vibration that would keep my mind in a positive mode.

I was determined not to think like the masses and become a programmed individual. Being programmed is simply thinking and believing everything that you are told. It's like living in another person's box. I was always conscientious of the thoughts that I was entertaining. Of course there are the negative thoughts that would sneak in when I would let my mental guard down. Catching those thoughts before they penetrate and permeate my mind and emotions would keep my mind in a higher percentage of positive thoughts. Being also conscientious of the body compelled me to be more selective of the types of food and water that I ingested. Taking good care of my body was very important for me. Exercise was an essential part of my life. A large chunk of my time was spent on moving my body.

I was always thinking that my body should be in a healthy state since it was the house, the living temple of the soul or spirit. My spiritual self became a high priority. I studied great spiritual teachers who laid the foundation for many to follow. In my early twenties I found the time to meditate. Meditation became essential to my well-being. It proved to provide basic care for all aspects of one's being.

Growing up in the traditional Christian church demonstrated that the boundaries and restrictions were stifling to my spiritual development. Passed from generation to generation, I was compelled to attend church services every sunday, as well as other days of the week. This was ongoing and constant. As far back as I can remember my brother and I attended church services. We were toddlers and it was ongoing until we reached adulthood. I continued in this vein well into my thirties. Teaching Sunday school, being an usher, choir member as well as performing a variety of duties in the church kept me very engaged in Christianity.

As I begin to seek God for myself and take personal responsibility for my soul's development, I began to grow spiritually beyond my imagination. I had read many books that were quite popular by the most noted ministers and pastors yet I never felt fulfilled. I always had a deep yearning as well as a knowing that there had to be more to God than what I had been told. Over time I would sit in the pews feeling like I was at a table where no real food was being served. I was past hungry. I was staving for more truth. I begin to study other religions and spiritual practices from around the globe. I took note that wherever a human was born on this planet was the determining factor of your religious or spiritual beliefs. Fear and guilt had poured from the pulpits warning the members to never look at other teachings. Getting over these programmed ideas was a real hurdle. There were so many families that I had grown to love that were part of the congregation. My first best friend that I loved like a sister belonged to this church. The church had grown in size as generations created a population swell within its corridors. Family members and other relationships had been built in this church. For me it slowly drifted into a huge social organization. I needed my spiritual needs satisfied.

It was a challenging decision to leave the friends that I had grown up with and come to love. The generational relationships tugged deeply within my heart. This was a lot to give up. I wrestled back and fourth attempting to make a decision that I would have to live with for the rest of my life. I felt like I was breaking a foundation that was strong and built by those who came before me. Breaking away from tradition is not easy. It can become a most difficult and trying experience. It certainly was for me.

I had anticipated the naysayers as well as those who would embrace my decision. I knew that there were those who would reject or even ostracize me. Yet I knew deep inside that this separation must occur for my own soul's growth. Yet a decision had to be made due to my thirst for spiritual knowledge that was no longer being quenched.

I reluctantly made a firm decision to leave the church. I found that I was gaining more knowledge on a daily basis than I would ever receive from the spiritual/religious teaching of one man or one doctrine. This decision became one of the most freeing choices that I have ever made. Over time I firmly decided that I should give divided yet equal attention to mind, body and spirit.

After a few years of being on my own I began attending a Unity based church. The teachings were based in Christianity but the belief that our lives were the outcome of our thoughts and actions intrigued me. The teachings were Bible based yet we read and studied books of the philoso-phers who set the standard for religion in America and Europe. I began researching other works by these authors that gave me deep insight into mankind's understanding of the souls of man and the soul and its functions.

Often, I reflected back upon my prior church family and felt deep emotions as too how little had been given in regards to taking responsibility of their own soul's care. Being a student of life for life, I always researched and read information and books that would offer me information that was more profound than my teachers. The foundation was laid but I built my spiritual growth brick by brick.

The wisdom that I pursued began to pursue me. The leaders of these organized religious orders over time began asking me for my insights, prayers and counsel. My goal was never rooted in competition. It was simply rooted in my soul's growth.

In doing so I found an inner awareness that allowed the trinity - mind, body and spirit to become my focus, as each would build upon the other. The total focus began to work in sync with each other. Mind, body and spirit seemed to be in perfect harmony.

My best friend from the church that I had known since we were toddlers was a good listener and took a deep interest in my spiritual journey. I could always bounce ideas and new insights into her listening ear. Understanding the path of my life as well as the twist and turns of my journey I found value in her capacity to listen.

My father was anchored in a strong belief in God. He believed in dreams as he was what I call a dreamer. Before entering kindergarten I remember my father would ask me every morning ritualistically, what did I dream. I would tell him my dreams and many times he would call his twin brother, my grandmother or other family members for me to share my dreams. He would then put the phone to my ear and direct me to tell the person on the line what I had dreamed. Being so young I did not understand at the time, that it was unusual for a parent to embrace such a quality. I have found that many parents suppressed this ability in young children and suppress this natural tendency. Not only did my father support my dream state, he embraced and honored it. Interpreting my dreams was as natural to him as having a cup of coffee.

As I grew in age his teachings increased. He taught me how to glean information from my dreams as well as how a dream would tell a story often being predictive or prophetic. Monitoring my dreams became very natural. Every morning as my father and I greeted each other one of us would ask the other, what did you dream? This was so common to me by the time I was a young adult I thought that everyone was a dreamer. I found this not to be true. My dreams had a prophetic nature. I would foresee incidents that would occur almost immediately. I often knew who would pass over and many times I was shown how the transition would occur.

Once I came into the understanding that my dreams could not simply be in the public domain, I became more guarded and secretive only sharing with with those whom I deemed close. I would tell my babysitter what to look out for regarding my children and other relevant information that supported their well being. On many occasions I had messages for neighbors, close relatives and others that found value in them. These dreams would just come and I welcomed them.

There was a time when I was a young adult I was being bombarded with so much information and insight into the lives of others that it had become overwhelming. I asked God to only show me that which I needed to know. I was quite firm with this request. I finally was relieved of some of the burden of knowing other people's business. At least I hoped that I was. Some of the dreaming ceased yet I was always alerted to dangers and sabotage by false friends and unscrupulous coworkers.

I felt quite harmonious with my dream state because my dreams would foretell many stories. They would forewarn me or alert me to issues and people that I should be cautious of. Of course I was interested in the character of those around me, yet I had no concern in regards to their personal lives. Dreams being natural to me, would be the topic or main idea in many of the books that had become my teachers.

Reading books based upon unusual phenomena introduced me to other unusual senses that are innate in mankind, that most are unaware, will not acknowledge, will suppress or simply ignore. I eagerly embraced many ideas that those in my environment knew nothing of or simply shunned, due to their religious teachings. Being stagnated in any area would never be my plight. At least that was my predominant thought.

I learned so much about the mind and spirit until I really was in a different place than those I interacted with, especially family members. As my social and professional arena grew, I found the lack of spiritual understanding was not limited to a religious order or doctrine, race or culture. Overtime I began to study the spiritual practices of those from the east. This was very exciting for me because it opened new doors of spiritual insight.

Over time I began to hear the still small voice within. It didn't come often but it came to redirect me so that I would avoid danger, accidents or other situations that were not for my ultimate good. As I reflect back sometimes I didn't listen, yet when danger was close the voice would become louder. Learning to listen to my inner voice became fascinating. I began to pay attention so that I would be able to discern and insure that any instruction or idea that I received would only be for the highest good.

I had a what was considered a good job. Over time due, to my rapid upward mobility my job became somewhat prestigious. Once I had a view of those who were in higher positions than I, it gave me a bird's eye view of their competencies or lack thereof. I had an inner feeling that I had skills that were more extensive than some of my superiors. I began to pay close attention to some of their capabilities and then often I noticed I had more. As I began to periodically seek advancement, I began to move up the rung of the professional ladder. Life was looking pretty good with so much potential until the day that changed my life came up on the horizon.

CHAPTER 2

AN UNWELCOME DIAGNOSIS

I had recently returned from traveling overseas where I had visited many countries. My body seemed to be having difficulties. While reflecting upon these travels at the time, I began to ponder the idea that maybe my internal time clock had been maladjusted due to traveling back and forth through many time zones. I thought that I had severe jet lag.

I desperately searched for supplements that could remedy this condition. I immediately purchased books relating to jet lag. While seeking I uncovered a powerful hormone called melatonin that I was not familiar with. This hormone had been utilized in regulating jet lag syndrome. I began to experience a tingling sensation in my feet. Somehow I had developed an awareness for my body as I paid attention to anything that seemed unusual or abnormal. I had dabbled in alternative medicine for a while using herbal teas as my medicine, as well as other alternative remedies.

I also relied upon the teachings of the early motivational and inspirational teachers, speakers and herbalist. There were many who spoke of mind over matter and inferred that a positive attitude could change your life. My goal was to direct positive thoughts into my body. I tried to ignore the tingling in my feet, believing that my positive thoughts and attitude would make the tingling go away. With the offering of prayers as well as meditation, healing seemed to be distant. The tingling overtime became a numbness.

I couldn't believe the enormous amount of guilt that I was feeling. Is this my self imposed punishment was my question to myself. The fact that I was sitting in a wheelchair was unimaginable, yet it was my reality. I sat solemnly wondering what the outcome of this visit would be and if it would change my life since I had no clue.

The neurologist utilized several different instruments to test my response to stimuli as the numbing climbed even further. After what felt like an interrogation, the doctor seemed to be looking into my soul. He made a firm decision and urgently informed me that I must enter the hospital immediately for further testing. I insisted that I needed to go home and pack a bag. The doctor quickly put an end to my idea of what I thought was necessary preparation for a hospital stay.

I did not want to enter a hospital but I knew that I didn't have an option. This was a most dreaded trip and my input was not requested. After entering the hospital more tests were administered. The instruments utilized for testing became more intense as well as extremely excruciating. It was a rarity to get a good night's sleep within those walls.

I was prescribed 500 milligrams of intravenous steroids every eight hours. At that point I did not know the ravishing effects of steroids upon the body and did not understand that steroids were considered a miracle drug but also an evil drug. I learned early in life to pray over my food. As the nurse hung a long clear plastic bag high over me and the liquid began to flow into my body, I felt devastated. I silently looked at the bag as the small voice within nudged me to ask God to extract the evil and only allow the good into my body.

Needles have always been something that I detested. I did not even like to look upon a needle. Now they had become a part of my day to day existence in this sterile, intimidating environment. I no longer felt like myself. The eyes that I looked out into the world with seemed to be stuck in a world that I had not known.

After a lengthy stay in the hospital these powerful drugs propelled me into steroid induced diabetes that created another physical condition that I certainly did not welcome. Being in a very weakened state with blood being constantly drawn caused me much discomfort.

Diabetes brought on more problems such as more blood being drawn, food modifications as well as other factors. Diabetes seemed small in comparison to the final diagnosis. Yet the devastating effects of diabetes had not been understood by me. The illness, discomfort and diagnosis became more complicated and devastating. It was quite troubling having to understand what was happening to my body. I was not aware that more bad news was too come. How does one wait patiently? Maintaing hope in such a condition was close to impossible.

The neurologist entered my room with a solemn look on his face and a serious demeanor. He began to explain the outcome of the multitude of tests that had been administered. I had an inner knowing as I braced myself for the bad news that I knew was coming. My diagnosis was transverse myelitis. I had never heard of such a disease, knew nothing of it's origin and had no idea how it would affect my physical body.

I learned that transverse myelitis is a condition that can rage havoc upon many systems within the human body. Receiving this diagnosis compelled me to research further into how this disease would present itself over time and if the possibilities of a cure would be available to me. There were many questions that I presented to the neurologist.

This disease generally dominates the central nervous system. Since the central nervous system controls the functions of the body, I began to look further into the functions of the operations of this system. The spinal cord is where transverse myelitis starts its journey.

Transverse myelitis is considered a very rare disease and can become ones death sentence. I accidentally came across an international transverse myelitis organization. Valuable information was available that aided my understanding of the disease. I had a belief the more I understood the disease, I would be able to save myself from its ravishes. My neurologist, along with a general practitioner, and a group of the top neurologists in my home state concluded that the previous diagnosis of transverse myelitis had done irreversible damage to my body. This diagnosis lead to many hospital stays. Too many to remember. This disease seemed to be a very fast-moving disease and in a matter of days I could not walk at all.

My hope began to diminish tremendously when a female doctor who spoke with a heavy accent came to my bedside. She smiled as she stood at the foot of my bed, well aware of my diagnosis and gently shook my feet through the blanket. She firmly looked at me and said "It is good that you checked into the hospital when you did, because you would have been dead in a day, maybe two." I did not understand or even consider the impact of her statement until, after a lengthy hospital stay, I was on a gurney in an ambulance headed to a nursing home.

As I reflect back, the nursing home was a short distance from the hospital yet the ride seemed to be the longest ride that I had ever taken. Those words continuously rang through my mind - "you would have been dead in a day or maybe two". I couldn't shake those words no matter how I tried, they stayed with me. There's a strange and deep feeling that is associated with a human hearing words such as death with your name attached. I was extremely weak in body, mind and spirit.

Weakness had overtaken the totality of my Being. I was bluntly told that I should prepare myself to never walk again. How do I prepare myself to believe that I could never walk again? Due to the diagnosis I did not respond, I had lost the will to fight. In less than two months time I could not understand how I could almost become a vegetable. My life was changing forever.

Being released from the nursing home was a real struggle for me. I was limited in my ability to walk but had no choice than to journey down this road with a positive attitude. My doctors had already presented me with a pessimistic outcome. The doctors had informed me verbally and in writing of the many restrictions that had been heaped up on me through this diagnosis.

I would have to stay out of the sun, which is exactly where I loved to be. I would have to stay away from chocolate, hot tubs, sex, certain foods as well as many other activities that made life worth living. I was also informed a number of times that I would never be able to walk again. Finally I stated to the neurologist that if he felt that I would never walk again, please never say it to me again. I knew that I had to take the high road as well as maintain a positive attitude. Having faith in a power greater than me was my saving grace.

After being released from the hospital I was mainly confined to the home. The medical services I received throughout the week were comprised of nurses and a physical therapist. The physical therapist did give me a little hope. As time passed on my doctors prescribed more potent drugs, each having their own unique side effects. I attempted to research each medication that I was prescribed. These medications gave me little relief from the sensations that were bombarding my nervous system. My nervous system was in a fragile state. The home care RN was charged with training me to use a needle to inject myself with a new potent drug. For her demonstration she utilized an orange. I was cringing inside as I watched her continuously inject the needle into the fruit.

Although I had many experiences now with needles through injections, infusions, testing and other traditional medical injections, I was not prepared to inject a needle into my skin. In fact the small vials of insulin still sat in my refrigerator unused. I hadn't come to grips with testing my own blood with a tiny prick of the finger. I tried to convince myself that I must adapt to the request in order to live with less pain and discomfort but I was not able to overcome the mental barrier that compelled me to take a strong stand against self injecting.

Reluctantly I had to explain to the neurologist upon my next visit as to why I refused to take additional drugs that were being prescribed to patients with my diagnosis. I had read about the side effects, informed the doctor and reframed from taking them.

CHAPTER 3

RETURNING HOME

Upon leaving the nursing home I was wheelchair bound in a handicapped minivan headed home. I distinctively remember upon hearing the brakes screeching from the many vehicles and how It felt like multiple knives with the sharpest points cutting through my skin. This was the most unusual and shocking experience for me. I would not have thought a feeling existed that caused such indescribable and excruciating pain. As I became more able to exit my home, I discovered that the finest drops of rain would feel like darts with very sharp tips hitting my skin. The pain was unbearable.

I became more familiar with handicap chairs designed for showers as well as walkers and canes. Not only is one affected physically, the psychological effects can be overwhelming and throw one into a state of darkness as well as hopelessness. The psychological effects were the most difficult to conquer. I believed if I could maintain psychological harmony by being positive, I would have a greater chance to regain my full health. Although my doctors strongly stated the devastation and progression of this disease, I found ways to ignore every negative idea.

Eventually I was diagnosed with multiple sclerosis (MS). I mustered up the will to fight the diagnosis. I was then diagnosed with depression and told that it was caused because I didn't want to accept the diagnosis of MS. I debated and took a firm stance that I was not depressed. Yet the doctors took a firm stance stating that I was. After being handed A box of depression medication stamped professional sample starter kit. I reluctantly accepted them and again left for home. My life was filled with doctor appointments, emergency room visits and hospital stays. Again I had to explain to the neurologist why I wouldn't take other experimental drugs that were being prescribed to MS patients. I informed the doctor that I had read and researched the side effects and would reframed from taking them. He then offered me three other drug options which I also refused.

The little free time that I had to think was utilized researching and pouring over information that could assist me in reaching a sense of wellness. Not only was my research aimed at healing my physical body, I delved into more spiritual ideals. Somehow I knew that I was going to be healed and the doctors were going to be in awe of my progress. Firmly anchored in this idea, with an understanding that nutrition plays a major role in those who are diagnosed with debilitating illnesses. I then put forth more effort towards mind, body, and spiritual wellness.

Which sufficient understanding of the nervous system and the myelin sheath to aid my research, I delved in. Many times I had several appointments in one week with a general practitioner or neurologist. Much of my allotted time was utilized by me asking questions regarding the the nervous system. I understood that the myelin sheath was comprised of a fatty substance that surrounds nerve endings, facilitates nerve impulses and has numerous functions. The neurologist gave me an example using electricity.

He said, "think of the myelin sheath as you would tape be it red or black, that is used in electrical wiring." The myelin sheath connects the nerves together as the tape connects electrical wires together.

He also stated that my myelin sheath was damaged or almost nonexistent throughout my nervous system. My question was how can I rebuild my myelin sheath? I was given no hope in the re-building of the myelin sheath. He seemed to believe that there was no hope for me. Yet I still maintained hope and faith that I would be healed somehow. I continued reading books and information that were very informative regarding the regaining of health. I began to incorporate every recommendation that seemed to fit my needs.

Spiritual ideals of healing became a serious aspect of my life. I studied miraculous healing from the past and present times. I began to seriously look at different types of healing prayer and affirmations. Since I had only been privy to a specific type of prayer that I had gleamed from Christian churches, I knew that I my scope of understanding of other religious teachings had to be expanded. Seeking to gain insight as to how their miracles were accessed as far as healing was concerned, I would incorporate different styles and means of prayer into my daily habits. My continuous seeking led me to the power of affirmations.

Through understanding the power and potency of affirmations, I was able to create and design my own. I found that when we design a prayer or affirmation specifically for an expected outcome, we generally find what we are seeking. Designing prayers and affirmations incorporates the personalized energy of the one who developed and created the words.

The level of potency lies within the energy that is poured fourth into each affirmation. The goal fueled with emotion gives substance and dynamic power to your words. I worked diligently toward my personal health and well-being and I attempted to not leave a stone unturned.

Those who knew of my diagnosis held so much fear for my future that often I had to assure them that I would beat the doctor's diagnosis, and I would win in the end. Although the odds seem against me, I used all of my mental might to beat back the negative thoughts and sorrow that was projected towards me. There were times when my body was seeming to fail me and I could only stand in my faith by expecting a miracle. I had many episodes from the MS. Many I ignored as I hoped they would leave or simply subside. I would silently suffer until the misery became overbearing physically or emotionally.

The doctors had often told me if I had specific symptoms that I should immediately go to the emergency room. I refrained from sharing my discomfort with friends and family for I knew they would suggest a hospital visit. Often being overwhelmed with physical suffering, I shared with those in my small circle the nature of my ailments. Naturally they pushed and begged for me to get to the emergency room quickly. This was always the last door that I wanted to enter. I knew the painful test as well as needles that awaited me. I was already busy trying to overcome the steroid induced diabetes.

The time arrived when the neurologist believed that I would simply deteriorate. A pre-emptive plan was put in place for me. It was believed that the disease would take its natural course. With all the tests and analysis that were available to my doctors, I believed that they had projected a time-frame as to when my body would no longer function. I had no visible signs of loss of kidney or the urinary system functions, yet I was given a referral to have a catheter placed in my body. There thoughts really weakened my resolve. It seemed to be another step backwards. I held the referral reading it over and over. It gave me much mental discomfort. I could not find the courage to go forward and it seemed to be leaving me fast. I made an effort to show up for the appointment yet I knew that I would not be emotionally able to have the procedure done.

Today I'm still grateful that I took a strong stance against this procedure. Even though having physical therapy at home gave me the ability to be mobile, with a walker or cane, the majority of MS patients eventually experience full paralysis.

My in-house RN informed me of an opportunity to get a van through the state. She gave me an overall review of the van and the different apparatuses and instruments that would give me an opportunity to drive myself once full paralysis set in. She explained that an instrument would be available in the van that would create movement so the turning of the neck would start the van, because it was designed with a lift wheelchair that supports the needs of a handicapped individual. The nurse seemed so happy for me that I had qualified for such a great gift. This did not seem like a gift that I should happily receive. I was very angry with the nurse but I never let on. She never knew of the effect that she left on me. This painted a more grim picture of what the future was to hold for me. When the nurse left my home I remember having a mental fight with myself that her words would not take root in my mind and rob me of my freedom or independence. I wanted my freedom back like a fish desires water.

As I continued to research and seek answers as to why I had MS, I began to believe that I did not fit into the criteria of one who should have MS. My doctor visits were weekly. Whenever I shared my belief with then, they constantly told me that I was depressed and that I did not want to accept the diagnosis. I cannot say if they were right or wrong regarding the depression.
I knew that the doctors were absolutely right, I did not want to except the final denominator.

Ingesting powerful steroids as well as a number of other extremely strong nerve and brain medications, made it more difficult to maintain and keep a positive attitude. When one is in the process of opening medicine bottles, counting pills and looking at six prone canes as well as walkers, it becomes an uphill climb. When all around you proclaim that the doctors know best and are constantly recommending that you follow their orders, it becomes difficult to live within the realms of positivity. I had been reading what was considered in my generation PMA (positive mental attitude) material. My mind had been saturated with this ideal. I motivated individuals as well as groups to adopt strategies that would lead to a positive mental attitude. This is before a famous woman brought it to the national front on television, and popular books were written on the subject.

As I look back, a positive attitude and outlook were deeply anchored in me. I kept the faith. I never believed that I would be totally paralyzed. I could not even conjure up an image of me being conquered by anything. I had read religious text and other literature that glued this ideal in me. As I look back I believe if I had tried to look on the dark or negative side I would not have been able to fully do so. My Spirit was strong, and I fought too keep it rooted in strength and truth.

What I did know for certain was that I had a mind, a body and a soul. With the body falling apart, I decided that the mind alone could not will the body whole again. I also understood that the body did not have the power to overcome MS. Yet I had a firm belief that the spirit would be able to empower the mind and the body to become whole again. I believed that I had to acknowledge the spirit as being separate but yet a major component of the whole. The still small voice would often be heard. I began to have a dialogue with the still small voice within. I began to listen more intently that I could learn the ways of the spirit.

This may seem far-fetched to those who have never had such an experience. In fact the masses may never have had these types of experiences, because most never quiet the mind. There are many distractions that are barriers to spirit communications. Such as television, radio, or other intentional and unintentional distractions. There are many variables that can grasp ones attention. Some may hold it for long periods of time that drown out the still small voice within as the attention is directed to lower value ideas. Yet the still small voice within can become a power broker as well as guide ones path down a road paved with success. As society looks more to external stimuli, the voice within that emanates from the innermost part of humans can be drowned out.

CHAPTER 4

TENDENCIES THAT RISE FROM THE SPIRIT

On Sunday in many houses of worship, we can see the spirit expressing itself in the human body. Witnessing the bodily contouring can be brief or lingering, often while uttering sounds not understood by the observers but known as shouting. The parishioners claim that the spirit took over their bodies. Then there are those who affirm that they spoke in tongues, while the spirit overtook them. Those who are not familiar will not understand the expressions being emanated through the speaking of tongues. Some who are under this influence claim that they understand the language and receive a message.

We cannot claim this to be false or untrue simply because we have not had the experience. Those who place limitations upon the spirit, basically limit themselves. There are a variety of religious practices that are expressive through spirit by a variety of means.

There are many phenomenas that are unknown to the larger society, and are rooted in ancient texts. Not being aware of their higher senses, the masses dwell mainly in the five physical senses, sight, hearing, taste, touch and smell. These are the senses that mankind uses on a daily basis and belong to the physical body. When any of these five senses are diminished, it reduces our ability to navigate effectively through life. Man has created many apparatus that may assist in restoring some of the senses when lost, yet they may be artificial.

There are many evolved or aware individuals who have tapped into, nurtured or embraced what is considered extrasensory perception (ESP). Generally known as clairvoyance or telepathy. It branches out into many facets. Basically information is perceived through senses other that the five physical senses. The five senses being accredited to the physical body. Extra Sensory Perception must be accredited to mind or spirit, since it is understood that there are three aspects of mankind-mind, body, and spirit. We credit the spirit with these profound innate natural tendencies. Many have accepted it as being naturally endowed and use it for their personal use and advancement, while there are those who benefit greatly from it in numerous ways. Yet the masses have been spooked or carry great fear of this wondrous innate ability.

Societal influences have demonized most unusual spiritual phenomena and have taught the masses that the works of the devil are at its foundation. However the elite and royals have historically benefitted, building kingdoms, amassing wealth and controlling the masses using these vast unlimited innate powers. The secrets of spiritual power have been hidden and kept amongst the royals the wealthy and the elite. History has taught us of the greater schools and the lessor schools. We cannot fail to consider the dark ages where no light of truth was acceptable to the rulers of that era. The threat of death loomed over those who dared to explore or share higher ideals. During this period little or no progress was made scientifically.

Those who utilize these senses use them in a great number of ways. They have been known for healing, manifesting or putting light upon a person's future walk in life. There are several classifications of ESP. This phenomena has not been accepted totally by the larger society. There are other phenomenas that are not accepted simply because the masses have not heard or been told of them. Yet as unusual as they are, unfamiliar phenomenas do exist.

We as a whole will probably never know or have an understanding of the depth and breath of the soul or spirit. These two terms I will use interchangeably. More people have become aware of these innate abilities and are using them to benefit themselves as well as others. Society will be using these extraordinary senses more due to evolution. We can see this in many areas of life. More are channelling and using these extra senses to inform and instruct the masses as to who they are, opposed to who they have been told they are.

Many awakened individuals have knowledge and wisdom that expresses itself from the spirit and through an open mind. Spiritually advanced teachers are sharing with humanity the ways and means as how to rebuild or remake themselves through spiritual laws. There are many known and understood spiritual laws that are infinite. As one steps up the ladder of spirit, each rung offers spiritual laws and wisdom that assists the individual as they ascend into heights of infinite possibilities.

Those who have not awakened into these possibilities may never experience what the spiritual realms have to offer. In order to experience these realms, one must remove all limitations that have been imprinted into their mental program. Of course we must always move forward with caution but must remain optimistic knowing deeply that our creator God has more to offer than mankind will ever know. A closed mind has self imposed limitations and remains rigid. When a mind is rigid it is unwilling to grow.

Planet earth is growing and evolving every day. As planet earth is our home we must grow to be in harmony and balance. Many lessor forms of life constantly adapt to their environment. As this planet shifts on its axis changes will occur. We too must adapt to our environmental changes.

CHAPTER 5

SPIRITUAL ATTACHMENTS
AND
EXCHANGES

Soul exchanges can occur in many different ways. This is a topic that is rarely discussed and have many taboos attached therein. Often it takes a brave individual to strike up a conversation of this nature amongst regular common folks. Generally when the masses think of a soul exchange, their thoughts immediately begin to consider a dark entity that brings mischief into the life of a human. Many immediately think of evil. Some believe that it is the work of satan.

Many think of movies that have portrayed evil entities screaming pro-fanities and leaving a trail of grief and suffering. Trickery or trickster spirits come to one's mind. Generally only negative ideas are considered when discussions or thoughts regarding a soul exchange are entertained. Holly-wood has set the tone as well as a frame of reference to many spiritual phenomenas. Souls outside of bodies have been portrayed as scary and frightful. Although many religions give credence to this experience, it has been difficult for the masses to accept the truth. A new soul can enter a body in several ways. Three of the ways I will be discussing soul ex-changes and attachments are through disincarnate spirits, soul braiding, and walk in souls.

When a soul has experienced what we call death, some believe that is the end of its existence on earth. The term transition is often used when the physical body no longer exists in the physical realm. Most believe that the soul returns to the higher realms. Many called these higher realms heaven.

When the soul exits the human body and is weighed down by an addiction, the soul may be unable or even unwilling to leave the physical realm. It is thought by many, in order for a soul to be reunited with God, the soul must ascend into and through various stages to reach its ultimate goal, the godhead. Many religious and spiritual leaders declare that the exiting soul begins its journey by seeking the light. Yet all souls do not have a desire to seek the light and some simply have lost their way. These souls detached from the body are called disincarnate spirits or souls. A sense of free will is still an aspect of the departed soul.

Souls can become lost or confused after exiting the body. There are many reasons for this type of occurrence. For example a violent death where the soul is abruptly expelled from the body or an accident that causes death, leaving the soul in a state of confusion. The prevailing emotions of despair at the time of death or deep sadness at the end of life may cause a soul to detour from its path towards the light. There are other human factors and unusual circumstances that can also cause this phenomena.

Disincarnate spirits are the ones that are generally portrayed in movies and mystery novels, whose motives are to thrust fear upon mankind. They are called ghosts, goblins, demons and other gory names.

Many disincarnate spirits have proven to be evil. There have been documented instances where families have been terrorized.

The Catholic Church, the foundation of Christianity, is known to have performed rituals called exorcisms. Exorcisms are performed to release humans from the gripes of disincarnate spirits that are causing pain and suffering in the life of the human. Exorcisms are still performed today but are not talked about as openly as they were in the past.

If disincarnate spirits are not real then why have a ritual to rid one of the effects of a spirit that remains here on earth? Disincarnate spirits do exist and can affect humans in all manners and ways. The entity who once had a human body was able to affect an individual, family, community, etc may choose to continue do so in the form of the spirit. All who willingly chose not to go to the light, were and are not dark spirits. There are those spirits that could not bear leaving loved ones behind. Many of this type had believed that they would stay with the loved one for a period of time, then pursue the light. They became stuck, earthbound and could not detach themselves to move forward and into the light. Often times there are husbands, wives or lovers who could not bear leaving their mates behind. They're also those who did not want to leave their children behind and they decided not to go to the light. These are generally those who are strong-willed and still want to control family matters.

Some mates who had become so accustomed to taking care of their lover and carried such deep love and commitment towards their well-being that they abandon the light to linger around the loved one until they are certain that one was being cared for, or was in a position to be cared for by another. Sometimes parents love or dominate their offspring to such a degree, that they do not trust them to make good decisions for themselves, therefore they will linger and not go to the light in an attempt to influence the offspring.

It is true there are dark entities that resist the light due to the physical senses that were very strong when they were in the physical body. When the soul leaves the physical body, some senses remain intact with the soul or spirit. These sensed emotions are the driving force of disincarnate entities. If certain senses were not carried over with the soul then there would be no desire for a soul to remain in the physical world. It would simply be a natural tendency for all souls that make their transition to go directly to the light. Not one soul would be left behind. There are many reasons that the disincarnate dark entities resist going to the light. Addictions may have taken over the life of the one who chose not to go to the light due to the love of them.

Alcoholics sometimes will not go to the light because they want to continue to stimulate their senses through those under the influence of alcohol. They linger around places that serve alcohol such as bars or homes where heavy drinking is a normal activity. They also hang around the homes where there are weakened humans addicted to alcohol.

The disincarnate entity will follow the addicted one by attaching to the human auric field, from place to place until it finds an opportune time to enter the human body of the alcoholic. The alive human alcoholic may fall into a drunken stupor. This would be a a favorable time for a disincarnate entity to enter the physical body of an alcoholic. Some spiritually evolved humans can see the attached entity within the auric field. Many have heard of, read about, or even understand the many facets of the human aura. The scientific community calls the aura the electromagnetic field surrounding the physical body. Instruments have long been developed to measure the intensity and vibrations of the auric field. Cameras as well can capture a picture providing the colors of the aura. Still others are able to see the colors within this field with the natural eye. It is described as being egg shaped by many. The width, depth and height of the aura varies from each individual.

Some spiritual practitioners have the eye to see an entity that has lodged itself into the auric field of a human. There are practitioners that have the ability to remove these entities and send them into the light. Of course that is a totally different and profound subject. An entity that attaches itself to one's aura slowly works its way into the body of an unknowing alive, breathing human host.

The entity can overtime propel or kick the other soul out and take over the human's body. Some entities will simply attach and stay with the host and change the course of the human's life. The entity also can influence the human to indulge further into the usage of alcohol. The family members, friends, or associates will say "the individual has changed so much that we hardly know him or her."

Many do not know the truth that they have spoken. The soul that once was known may have moved on or may be dominated by an entity. They are now interacting with a new soul that has become the essence of the person that they once knew.

There is also what is known as a violent take over. This generally occurs when one is in an alcohol induced condition that we term as a very drunken or inebriated state. Often the alcoholic has passed out. In this state an entity will violently intrude into the body of its victim. When the victim awakens he generally has no recollection of this takeover. If there is a memory of this event it is cast-off as a nightmare, hallucination, or a figment of the imagination.

Oft-times the victim is aware that something has occurred but he does not know or have the words to frame such an occurrence. Even if re-membered, the victim has no words to adequately describe such an event. If the victim remembers, his dilemma may be difficult to describe out of fear of being ridiculed. What terms would one use to describe such an episode and what words could one use to explain such a take over? Who would lis-ten and who would understand? He or she simply continues to live in an al-coholic state and continues to steadily decline in mind, body, and spirit. The person has now become a permanent host to an alcohol infused entity. The victim's life is wrecked, as the victim begins to disrupt and wreck the lives of others. Those who interact with these individuals will find their rela-tionships damaged or broken.

There also remains in the physical world disincarnate entities that were drug addicts while they were alive in a physical body. They like to roam around those who are addicted to meth, heroin, cocaine, or other drugs of choice. They linger in drug houses where drugs are being made, distributed or used. Similar to the alcoholics, the drug addicted disincarnate entities seek out easy prey. Those who are in a drug induced stupor are easy to find. These entities hang around until the time is ripe to strike it's unknowing victim. These disincarnate entities will find a home in a rehab center or other sites such as a homeless shelter. Anywhere drug addicts can be found, there will be disincarnate entities waiting to pounce upon it's unknowing victims.

This is the main reason that one should protect himself when visiting places of this nature. It is best to steer away totally from places where one knows that drugs are being utilized in any fashion. Many times a person that is clean and has never used drugs can begin to work as a professional to assist these addicts yet become addicts themselves.

This occurs due to their lack of knowledge of the invisible enemies lurking in these places where addicts seek assistance. Prayers, affirmations, usage of the white light etc, for protection should always go forth prior to visiting these places, to insulate one from a destiny of addiction through attachment. The fate of those who are a victim to this type of entity is usually a downward spiral of darkness, despair, pain and suffering.

The majority of people do not have a clue as to what is lying in wait in these dim, dark places, ready to pounce upon an unsuspecting victim. Disincarnate entities can and do travel from one person to another. This is why it is not wise to interact unguarded with those who have addictions. When in close proximity to another human one may not know what is lurking or should I say who is lurking in that one's auric field. Since one's auric field extends several feet away from its physical body it can overlap with another's auric field. An entity can simply merge into another's auric field with ease. There are spiritual practitioners who are skilled, well aware of these entities and utilize many techniques to detach dark entities from alive humans.

Rarely does one think of sexual addictions. There are entities that left the physical plane and had no desire to go to the light due to their sexual addictions. The physical sensations of sex took control of the alive human being. When the time came for the soul to make its transition into the light it made a choice to stay and linger closely to those who love the pleasures of sex. Those who have compulsive sexual thoughts, or cannot manage their sexuality, drifting from partner to partner maybe exposing themselves to a disincarnate.

Despite negative consequences, sexual addicts will put their family, finances and even their life at risk for sexual pleasures or sexual satisfaction. Entities that harbor this addiction want to continue the pleasures of the sexual experience. After leaving the physical body, the disincarnate spirit will not go to the light. They seek people who have this very addiction and find ways of satisfying their own senses by lingering around those who have the same addiction.

As society has emerged and increased into a more sexual culture, sexuality has expanded. Phone sex, strip clubs, prostitution and all manners of sexuality has become acceptable.

Entities linger in many places, even in individual homes were certain sexual practices that are deviate are being performed.

Disincarnate entities attach themselves to unknowing victims time and time again until the victims fall deeper into the clutches of the down spiraling acts of sexual deviation, not aware that an entity has been the force and influence into very dark sexual acts that may even lead to death.

There are still other addictions such as food. The same rings true for food addicts. When one loses control over his consumption of food, he can easily step into it an addictive behavior, where food rules. Disincarnate entities who had food addictions when alive and still desire to stimulate the senses will attach to those who are addicted to food. This is not as common as other addictions.

I would be remiss not to mention disincarnate entities who remain earth bound to gratify their desires for revenge, where they may attach themselves to those who they knew and despised while alive. The hate and resentment harbored by these entities are projected upon the unknowing victim as the victim is tortured in a variety of ways.

This may range from being disturbed during sleeping hours, the slamming of doors, items flying off of tables and other disruptive situations occurring where the source of the disturbance is not seen or understood. There are a variety of ways were individuals who are a host to these entities are made very uncomfortable. Some may believe that they are having an unlucky streak, etc. One can be drained of his energy, finances, and other valuables. Divided relationships can also be the results of these attachments.

Those who have been extremely violent and vicious hang around and attach to victims that they may continuously carry out these ill deeds. We often claim that the person has a mean or evil spirit.

Generally the goal of these types of entities is revenge. If one wonders why they are stuck in dysfunctional relationships, a low income job, or simply cannot produce at the level that they are capable of, they should look deeper into what may be holding them back. One must simply understand when something is wrong then something is not right. Discovering what is not right may lead one to look into deeper possibilities. If one delves into the spiritual aspect of life, the answers may be found.

When one concludes that help cannot be gained through traditional treatment options, it is recommended that one should seek out spiritual professionals who have had success in treating what is called disincarnate entity attachment. Traditional professionals and schools of higher learning have not readily embraced and developed techniques, therapies or sufficient research to assist those who suffer from such a phenomena.

When the body is out of harmony or balance, the body must be nurtured or tended to by those who understand the nature of the bodies biology, such as medical doctors or alternative medical practitioners. When one's mind seems to be out of balance or harmony, one will seek professional practitioners, and counselors who have a clear understanding of the function of the mind. Be it a psychologist or psychiatrist. When the spirit or soul has a dysfunctional aspect it must be addressed through and by those who understand the nature of the spirit and its many facets. As humans evolve into a deeper understanding of the nature of the spirit, society will become more whole.

Hundreds of books have been written on near death experiences (NDE). Individuals who died and came back to life have given testimony to the events that took place. Most of these deaths were witnessed by medical professionals whose lives were under their care. Some passed over while surgery was being performed and others under different circumstances. A major accident could have been the basis of the near death experience. There are thousands of people across the globe who have tasted death or touched death's doors as there are numerous documented accounts of the afterlife.

These accounts are considered credible because they occurred to people from all walks of life. Some of the highest and most respected in their given fields and some were just common people. One thing that they attest to which seems to be a common thread is that they all left their bodies and were able to see their bodies in a deathly state as they hovered above it. A major similarity that they generally confirm is that they saw a light, a bright light, as they travel to it in spirit form. Most who returned claim that they saw the highest of the hierarchy of their religious belief system. If one expected to see St. Peter, he saw St Peter, if one believed that he would see Jesus, Buddha, Allah or any other deity that they believed in is who they were greeted by.

Many tell the story of being in such a peace filled state that they wanted to stay. Believing that work was left undone, they returned to their body to carry out these duties. Many also state that they saw loved ones who welcomed and were embraced by them. Some indicated that they communicated with higher beings of light who expressed that they must remain on the plane of the living for future work as they were allowed to return.

When these individuals return to earthly life they generally have a great change in their perspective of life as well as their purpose. Upon returning to their bodies they have a new and different outlook in regards to humanity and the planet earth itself. Belief in a power greater than themselves has increased. This occurs because they no longer look at life from a simple physical existence. Upon returning intact with life force, many claim to have returned with newly found skills. For them the skills sprang from the spiritual side of life. Many return with the ability to heal, clairvoyance, clairaudience, or a number of qualities connected to intuition or the spiritual side of life.

Marvelous works have been provided by many who have experienced a near death experience. Untold numbers have benefited from the assistance and knowledge that these individuals have provided to mankind. Scientific research has supported much that has been said here. Science has demonstrated thru research the approximate amount that the soul weighs as it has been analyzed while leaving the human body.

The Western world lags far behind in giving credence to the functions of the soul or spirit. In the east there are countries rooted in ancient text and historical records of the spirit and are still embraced or adhered to. This knowledge has been passed down from generation to generation. These teachings and insights have slowly emerged into western studies. Even certain European countries have made advances in spiritual understanding, more so than America. We have been fortunate to have such a melting pot in America that many other cultures have brought their traditions and thoughts of the spirit and merged them with the west. Some practice these traditions diligently today.

Soul Braiding is yet another phenomena. This occurs when a new soul merges with the living human soul. An agreement is made between the two souls to have the exchange. The agreement may be made prior to the embodiment or the birth of the receiver of the soul as well as after. There are many reasons for soul braiding. The receiver soul may have a strong desire to fulfill its purpose on planet earth yet does not have the resources or skills to accomplish it. The desire is usually of a high order. The new soul brings the knowledge or information that is necessary to access the original soul's goal. The new soul will carefully and strategically braid with the host receiver's soul. They generally contribute much to the development or evolution of those on planet earth. Many times the receiver is not aware of this occurrence while in the process of the exchange.

Their is a blending of the personality, character, emotions, values ,morals, etc. The new soul has a structure or framework to merge with. This somewhat eases the adjustment process. The existing soul has the challenge of adapting to the new soul. One may feel out of sorts as the blending takes place. It will vary from person to person. These entwined souls begin to operate as one. The blueprint laid out by the original soul gives the new soul the building blocks to weave itself into. This is not an easy task for a human to encounter. Major as well as minor adjustments in the thought processes as well as the personality must be tackled.

The original soul, if balanced can bring in immeasurable gifts to aid societies' ills as well as aid this planet's evolutionary process. The abilities of the soul have been under estimated in its breath and width. Today certain segments of society believe that we humans are multidimensional Beings. This means that we humans are more than we have known ourselves to be. It is now understood that wherever our consciousness is we are there. This is how we can be in one place yet have an effect in another.

Man has placed limitations on the power and presence of the soul. Through attention and soul searching we will discover more of the magnificent abilities that are comprised and housed in the eternal essence of the soul of mankind.

I shall finalize the different phenomenas that can and have affected humans from all walks of life, irregardless of race, culture or social standing. These unusual phenomena's have been documented historically from ancient text to prophets of today. Simply because one has not heard of these phenomenas does not rule out the fact that they exist.

CHAPTER 6

A WALK IN SOUL DEFINED

Now we shall discuss what I consider the most difficult and challenging soul exchange. It is called the Walk In Soul. Many view the walk in from a negative point of view due to their lack of knowledge and insight into the fortunate ones who have had this experience. A walk in generally occurs when the physical body is in a weakened state. The weakened state due to an accident, illness, depression, a desire to commit suicide, a coma and a number of declining physical or mental issues. A broken heart can be the catalyst for this unusual phenomena. There are many variables that may cause suffering in the human body. A damaged body can be a prerequisite to a walk in soul exchange.

The walk-in can occur at an accident scene where the body of the individual is not damaged beyond repair. It can occur on an operating table while one is undergoing surgery as well as in a hospital room where it seems like recovery should be taking place. It can occur when life is hanging by a thread. A walk in exchange can occur in the home of an emotionally drained individual who no longer has a desire to live. This exchange can occur in the most unusual as well as common places.

Spiritual teachers, clairvoyants and evolved non-traditional spiritual teachers have indicated that an agreement was made prior to a walk in soul exchange and are often made prior to the receiver's physical birth.

Understanding these exchanges will offer our ever evolving society an opportunity to glimpse into the infinite world of spirit.

Over the last few centuries many well-known prophets, seers, and sages have passed down knowledge that was gained through spiritual communications. Many sought this knowledge and there were others that the knowledge simply found them. There are characters portrayed in most religious doctrines that embodied these spiritual tendencies. Many called these tendencies that allows one to see into the past, or future a gift from a higher power. There are those that believe these tendencies to see beyond the six senses as innate in mankind.

Depending on the religious or spiritual teachings that one adheres to generally determines the level of understanding and openness one may hold relevant to the realm of spirit. Many scientific findings were discovered by spiritually minded scientist who used the spirit realm in seeking answers to the most perplexing questions. Many archaeological discoveries were uncovered due to the knowledge that had been passed on from those who had the ability to tap into the spiritual realm without using the basic physical five senses. How else could archaeologist know and understand where to look for certain historical artifacts, records, relics, etc.

There are ancient texts, religious teachings as well as prophets of old that have described the phenomena of the walk in soul. This alludes to the fact that walk in souls have been occurring historically. Some of these teachings were hidden from the masses or just overlooked. Today many advanced individuals utilize the works of these prophets to predict occurrences that may happen in today's world where as they can plan or even profit from these predictions.

To be aware of knowledge long before the masses can place one in a powerful position.

I had known for many years that I was a walk in soul as I documented many of the changes that had occurred in me. Yet after many years of being a walk in I am still discovering a variety of expansive truths as to who I am as well as the diversities that are common amongst walk ins.

Many of the traits that I thought to be common for years amongst humans, I have found not necessarily to be true. One being the constant wondering why others did not have the understanding or knowledge that I embodied. Although I had always been a seeker as well as an avid reader, I have discovered that these characteristics were not common to most humans. I had a tendency to label the others as lazy thinkers, which I found not to be true. As we move forward with these discussions , you will understand why.

From this point on I will begin to use the terminology "from my understanding, from my knowledge, from my insight". As using these words you will better understand that this information has come from the realm of Spirit or from synchronicity that led me to a book, a teacher or informative symbols, etc.

Only a few have heard or know of the term walk in soul, less is known of the gifts that a walk in bears. Walk ins are privileged to knowledge, wisdom and information that flows from within or from a higher source. Information that walk ins embody is usually of a higher spiritual order. Where does the new soul come from, where did it abide while not in a physical body?

The new soul comes from a higher realm, another dimension. It brings within its essence wisdom, information and advanced knowledge. Information that has not necessarily been available within the third dimensional realm that planet earth is. Higher realms do exist, quantum physics supports this ideal. Since a soul never dies, it must live in a realm higher than planet earth.

Due to the shift occurring on planet earth as well as the earth ascending, there are souls waiting in the higher celestial spheres to take on a life in a physical body. There is excitement and joy in the spiritual realms as to the ascension of planet earth. Ascending from a planetary perspective is a metaphysical term that describes or defines planet earth's shedding of the old and bringing in the new. Some believe that the collective consciousness of humanity is raising into a higher field, and there are those who firmly believe that the human DNA is being modified and upgraded due to the cosmic and galactic energy being poured into this planet.

It is common knowledge that the moon affects the tide, liquids, a woman's menstrual cycle as well as the emotions of mankind. Without study and research one would never know the other effects that the moon and the sun have on humans.The moon being a lunar celestial body while the sun being a solar celestial body, we can understand why under certain phases of the moon there is an increase of deeds that are fueled by the emotions.

Law enforcement professionals have documented that there is an increase in crimes of passion under specific phases of the moon especially the full moon. Mental-health practitioners have informally labeled clients who have a specific mental dysfunction as lunatics. Why is the prefix luna being utilized as luna is associated with the moon?

There is still much mystery surrounding the influences of the moon upon the behavior patterns of animals as well as humans. How often have we seen pictures depicting a full moon in the background while a wolf is howling? The wolf is used to symbolize the animal kingdom being affected by the celestial body, the moon. Farmers of old planted and gathered crops under different phases of the moon. Almanacs have been utilized as a guide by farmers to determine the best phases. Babies have been weaned according to the phases of the moon as well as other issues relevant to life force.

Most people understand, believe, and have been educated to the fact that the sun being a solar force, affects the human body in many ways. We know that the sun pours forth vitamin D that is necessary to sustain a healthy body. There are some cultures that understand that lying in the sun at a specific times can cause the body to heal and eradicate certain bacteria or viruses. Some feel renewed after sunbathing. The sun is known to give energy and zest to life. The lack of sunshine can cause a number of physical, mental and emotional ailments. Lighting systems have been developed to depict the sun's energy. These lighting systems have assisted those who suffer from a lack of sunshine. Many diseases have been identified from a lack of sunshine such as seasonal defective disorder (SDD).

If the medical society has uncovered specific illnesses due to a lack of sunshine, we can only guess what the benefits the sun pours out into humanity. In understanding how two celestial bodies affect mankind. One would think that other celestial bodies can and do affect our well-being. There are a number of celestial bodies that are common such as planets, stars, asteroids, comets, etc. Ever wonder why the creator of all life has allowed the sun and moon to affect humans and the necessity of it? I have a feeling that all celestial bodies affect us in numerous ways. Some of the heavenly bodies affect humans more profoundly than others. With a little research and information we cannot rule out the effects of the system of worlds that exist above us but yet are within our reach.

Evolved spiritual individuals are claiming that children have been born that have a very different DNA over the last decades. There are many who are highly regarded and well-known who have written and authored books regarding these newly developed types of beings. Some of these children who are adults now have been labeled indigos, crystals, star seeds, etc. This leads us to believe that these changes are originating from something, but what? There are prophets of old from every continent who have projected the ideals from walk ins to new children populating the planet. Some prophets were known to go into a deep trance where they were able to access knowledge from higher planes. Many study their predictions today and find them to still ring true. Many of these predictions indicated that there would be walk in souls that would come from a higher dimension to aid and guide humanity into the next evolutionary step.

If all religious teachings indicate that the soul never dies we must know that there must be a place where the soul continues to live. We must ask ourselves if the souls continue to live what do these souls do and what are their capabilities?

It has become a common understanding that professional mediums are available to communicate with loved ones that have passed over. Horse whisperers as well as animal communicators have become a sought out profession. How do these mediums develop a means of communications with the so-called dead? We may not understand the intricate details but the proof has been in the satisfaction of those who have utilized their services.

The information provided should offer us satisfactory knowledge that something exist in the unknown that can and does affect every aspect of the human from the physical, emotional as well as spiritual.

We have been taught and programed to embrace many fears relevant to the spiritual aspect of the human. These range from ghost to poltergeist that generally look and perform disgusting deeds.

We must not become immersed in the negative only. We must take a look at the positive aspects of spirit that we need not fear. I think a lifesaver is a very positive aspect of the Spirit or soul, especially when it brings in a higher dimension of love, compassion, understanding, and insight into the need's of the people of planet earth. The gifts that walk in souls bring are countless.

CHAPTER 7

WALK IN SOULS
AGENDA

My understanding is that the new walk in souls have an agenda that they would like to carry out to assist mankind during this evolutionary period. We believe when a newborn emerges from its mother's womb a soul enters that body. It becomes the original soul of that infant. We have been taught that a human is born with a soul, and that is the only understanding in regards to the soul. There is deep and passionate debate as to when a newborn baby takes on a soul. The question has become, does the baby emerge from its mothers womb intact with a soul or does the soul enter the new born as it exits the mothers womb? The masses have limited understanding in regards to the soul's entry into the human body. This demonstrates the limited knowledge that is known or limited information that has been handed to humanity.

Many souls (walk in soul) that await to enter a body are well advanced and do not want to complete the process from infancy into adulthood. Time is of essence and the need of the wisdom that these ancient souls bring to planet earth is crucial. I will reiterate that an agreement has already been put in place, within this lifetime or prior too. Within the spirit world time is not separated into the past, present and future. It is considered eternal time. Operating within eternal time allows one to see or experience the past, present or future within the now timeframe. These awaiting souls operate within the idea of eternal time not linear time that the masses of humans live within.

There are many circumstances that may occur in the life of humans whereas a walk in may enter a human body. From my spiritual understanding, when a human body is damaged yet repairable, the new soul will enter that physical body. Giving up the will to live is another, while overwhelming despair can be a precursor. There are many unknown and untold experiences that can cause the transfer of a walk in soul. We humans are not privy to all of the variables surrounding this highly exalted exchange.

Once the complete exchange has occurred the new soul is operating harmoniously in the new host body, it begins to complete any unfinished business that the old soul needed to address. The old soul generally offers skills as well as a spiritual foundation that is developed to the degree that it can be placed in alignment with the goals of the new walk in soul. This is necessary that the new soul can quickly put it's own agenda in place. The new walk in soul wants to be about its business of serving the needs of humanity. In the last three decades more walk in souls have entered planet earth that any other time.

In 1987 an astrological event occurred called the Harmonic Convergence which began the shift of the collective consciousness of the people of planet earth. Those who are more interested in this event will find many interesting, and thrilling writings on the topic. This event was predicted by ancient civilizations, astrological professionals, and spiritually minded humans who claim that an unusual configuration of planets was identified as well as initiating the beginning of earth's planetary shift.

The Mayan calendar, prophecies and other interesting historical works were utilized in researching this unusual planetary alignment. Many beliefs have emerged regarding this astrological event. The collective human consciousness supposedly has been affected. This event has been the catalyst that has created knowledge and information to be accessible to humans in regards to this evolutionary leap. It is evident by the increase in knowledge coming forth publicly by a large number of individuals who claim to be receiving knowledge from spiritual discernment, Arch Angels, Ascended Masters, extraterrestrials and other Cosmic Beings. There are also many who claim to be in touch with other planetary beings. How ever one views these unusual happenings on planet earth, it can be found to be a very exciting time.

A walk in soul has no bias in regards to race, sex, cultural, social or economic factors. From my understanding there are many souls excited to have an opportunity to participate in the evolution of planet earth. So much that there is a long waiting line.

From outer space planet earth is seen as one of the most beautiful inviting planets in the galaxy with it's wondrous beautiful waterways and green forestries that give off a beautiful panoramic view. Planet earth's electromagnetic field also affects other planetary systems.

Once the new soul has entered a physical body often major adjustments must be made. One of the most intrusive as well as most difficult positive soul exchanges that happens is when the new soul enters a physically challenged body. Positive because it can be a lifesaver, as well as give the human a second chance at life with a new zest for living. It can also cause a modified physical appearance without altering the physical features. The new walk in soul must endure the full responsibility of adapting to the new physical body and all that it bears.

The the new soul must adapt to the character, personality, language, nuances, emotional attachments and other aspects of the old soul which is the most difficult task. Humans are such complex beings that one can only imagine the process of fully adapting to the totality of another human. Adjustments are constantly being made, be it mental, physical, emotional or spiritual.

Metaphysicians and other spiritual teachers would even suggest that the subtle bodies must make an adjustment also. Subtle bodies being comprised of multidimensional layers within the human auric field. Some believe that the subtle body is made of light, thought or pranic energy.

There are still those who believe that this energy field is multi dimensional and reaches as well as connects to the Godhead or Creator.

There are those who have the ability to see the visual form of each subtle body in distinguished patterns as well as outlined boundaries. Ancient texts bear witness to this field that extends from the physical body of mankind. Scientists have highly developed instruments that can measure the intensity of this field surrounding humans. All of these complexities must be systematically adapted and adjusted, to have what is commonly thought of as a normal fit.

This is necessary that the body can maintain balance, harmony and wholeness. If this balance does not occur the imbalance can be seen by outside observers and considered a physical or mental deficit. Time constraints will vary for each individual to find harmony and peace in this unusual phenomena. If the physical body was not ill the transition can be seamless. Where the host of the walk in soul may never know that a soul exchange has taken place.

The person may feel that a change has taken place and never ponder the possibilities of what might have occurred. Levels of awareness may be the determining factor as to what and how much is remembered in regards of the soul exchange. Most humans who have a walk in soul are not aware that they are. Reflection and pondering ones life may offer a clue that a soul exchange may have taken place.

Generally when unusual spiritual happenings occur, most know nothing of the subject and have no idea as to how to relate to incidences that are different from the normal societal experiences. Therefore meaningful conversations regarding these types of events are never a main topic, hardly discussed and rarely understood.

There are times when the original soul will linger and assist the new soul in the changeover. This will aide the new soul during the adjustment period. The original soul can leave the body abruptly when the new soul moves in. This happens when the walk in was initiated due to the old soul no longer having the desire to continue with it's life. The person may have been suicidal or given a death sentence through a medical diagnose or accident. Life's issues may weigh heavily on an individual that drives and compels the person into suicidal tendencies.

One must be clear that we cannot activate, demand or request a walk in soul. The walk in soul chooses you. You cannot choose a walk in soul. I cannot impress this strongly enough. One cannot create a scenario such as an accident or suicide that would draw a walk in soul unto themselves. A walk in soul discovers the human body for the transfer. Long spiritual observation and effort is put in place well before a body is identified for such an exchange. We have seen those who were deep in the throngs of depression who felt that they had nothing to live for and stepped close to the edge of taking their own life, become new individuals.

When we see those who have stepped firmly out of the depths of this despair, make a complete turnaround and have a love as well as purpose for life, this may be due to a walk in soul. There was a time that I believed that a devastating illness must occur before a walk in takes place. I have since gained a new understanding. Walk ins can happen under many different scenarios and circumstances. My thinking today is those who have been under the domination of an abusive spouse may finally be freed from this slow emotional death into the freedom and light of a walk in soul.

Many have consciously or unconsciously thought or stated "my guardian angel was with me" when they were faced with certain difficulties. For those who are nonbelievers that don't believe in help from the other side. You must ask yourself the questions who was this guardian angel? Where did the guardian angel originate from? Where does it abide? Why did it assist me? Why can't I feel its presence every moment instead of on certain occasions? All of these questions have answers. If you are not an atheist then you are a believer in a higher Being. If you were aware of that something or some unseen force assisted you in times of trouble then you are a believer of the presence of celestial beings. If you believe in angels or

Arch Angels, you already believe in Celestial Beings. We must know that there is a hierarchy and structure and order in all of creation.

We can take a look from the plant life to the animal life to the human life and up the ladder to the Celestial Beings and onward and upward to the god head or creator. There is a system of worlds within worlds. If these worlds or systems were not organized there would be complete chaos. When there is no definite order or boundaries, all systems would haphazardly fall together in a chaotic soup. Nothing identifiable as a separate whole would exist. There are definite realms and boundaries as well as dimensions that have organized energy fields being fed by the Creator all that is necessary to sustain each separate yet whole.

It is not my purpose to convince anyone of the infinite possibilities within the spirit realm. My intention is to present that which I believe to be true. I firmly believe that what is true for one today can change as one begins to add new knowledge and information to their old truths, then a new truth emerges. As this new truth emerges we become a new human being. Humanity is evolving right in our face. To remain relevant in this age we much open our minds to the new.

Terms such as star-seeds, indigo children, crystal and rainbow children are becoming a common name to describe the new generations who have and are entering planet earth. They bring fourth a new philosophy.

They came to change the very nature of humans on this planet. There are those who claim the DNA of these children is different than generations past. This information and understanding is slowly but certainly being researched by some of the best minds.

Many understand the functioning of the human body as well as its nutritional needs. Yet when we change or modify our eating, drinking, and habitual thinking, we transform ourselves and become a new revised human being. When humans cannot or do not choose foods that are considered health giving the human body suffers. Many humans suffer through drought and famine that may effect an entire region. Lives are lost from lack of access to food. The body suffers in many ways when food cannot be assimilated or digested through what is considered the normal process of physically eating.

The medical society has mechanisms that are utilized to sustain life intravenously. To sustain a good healthy physical body nutrition is a necessary component. When the physical aspect of a human declines, we generally seek out a medical professional to aid us in gaining our good health. Research indicates that the human boy is comprised of 70 to 80 percent water. Every function in the body is dependent on water to perform its task. Without water the body will immediately begin to decline. The quality of our drinking water makes a vast difference in the quality of our health. Without clean toxic free water human bodies begin to dehydrate or devolve and lose it life force and vitality. There are many factors that can effect our good health. If the body becomes ill, we seek medical attention to remedy the condition, again generally a medical doctor.

Mental illness has a wide reaching affect upon the minds of humans, such as depression, anxiety, ptsd, autism, alzheimer's, etc. There are too many to mention. Many have seen the devastating effects of mental illness upon the lives of friends, coworkers, family members and loved ones. Mental illness can be caused by many factors such as a brain injury, biological factors, and exposures to toxic chemicals. Serious medical conditions at times are the cause of mental decline. Behavioral issues are often rooted in mental illness.

Research has indicated that our thinking can influence our physical bodies in profound ways. This suggests that our thoughts are powerful and can cause and increase in good health or a decline. When we begin to take charge as well as the responsibility of our prevailing thoughts it is believed that we can change our physical bodies as well as our emotional wellbeing. Although when mental decline is recognized humans will generally seek out or are referred to a mental health professional such as a psychiatrist, or psychologist, who understands the functioning of the mind.

Down through the ages mankind has attempted to understand the soul or spirit of man. Prior to the development of the alphabet man has attempted to describe their ideas regarding the abilities and capabilities of the soul. This was documented through pictures and symbols such as hieroglyphics. Archeologists today are seeking artifacts that share a history of the beliefs of the ancient peoples of planet earth. Defining the most inner working of the soul or spirit is a quest that will be ongoing as long as there is life.

Every generation has made gains in understanding, defining or interpreting the ways of the spirit. The deeper that mankind has a glimpse of the spirit the more complex the spirit becomes.The soul has been said to live forever. All religions claim that the soul or spirit is the most important aspect of man, as there are well over a thousand documented religions.

Society has positioned humans to individually rely on their personal resources for food for the body as well as medical care for it. The financial responsibility for the mental wellness of the individual is reliant upon ones personal resources also. Yet there has been an effort to captivate the soul or spirit of man through religion. Rarely are we told that we should be or are capable of being responsible for our very own souls development. History dictates that we humans have been evolving for millions of years. The soul has evolved also. A lifetime of research of the functioning and components of the soul will never be discovered. As researchers pass on, souls are continuously evolving. We can never know all there is to know of the soul or spirit.

Many believe that we humans need spiritual food such as prayer, positive thinking, meditation as well as contemplation. It is thought when we feed our spirit or soul with this type of nourishment its capacity grows and expands. As the spirit expands it has the capacity to utilize certain powers that are embodied in the essence of the soul.

When lacking of any spiritual nourishment, accordingly our spiritual selves began to shrink, suffer, devolve or become dormant in direct proportion to its famine. The nature of man being mind, body and spirit, all three components should be in balance to have serene harmony. When one finds that their suffering, lack of growth or peace is disturbed and it is determined not to be of the physical body or the mind, one should then look at the spiritual aspect of the human. The medical and mental professionals may be good for the body and mind but not astute in the wellness of matters of the spirit.

We then must seek more than a religious teacher who trains one in regards to a doctrine, unless he or she is astute in the nature of healing on a soul level. There are many professionals who have developed a deep understanding of the multifaceted aspects of the soul. They can assist in the healing process and matters of the spirit. There are many techniques and modalities that are available from dedicated Spiritual healers that can discern the discomforts of the soul and assist in the healing process. Spiritual healers have been responsible for recoveries that are considered miraculous. When difficulties can not be remedied from the biological or mental aspect, I recommend a spiritual practitioner.

Each walk in soul transfer is uniquely different. The transfer can be accomplished within various time frames. My understanding is that the walk in soul transfer is assisted by advanced beings from a higher dimension. Their duties are to insure that disincarnate entities do not interfere with the process. Their interaction with the newly entering soul and the soul exiting the physical body are given proper care and counsel. These higher dimensional beings ease the process or transfer by alleviating the fears and trauma that can be associated with the soul exchange. It has also been written that these higher beings assist in the severing of the silver cord. This invisible silver cord is considered our spiritual bodies lifeline attached to the physical body. Different belief systems have names for the cord relevant to their teachings.

As a newborn baby is born, the umbilical cord is cut from it's mother. At the end of a physical life the cord is served in order for the soul to be released from the body. The same must be done for the departing soul in a walk in soul exchange. These beings aid in that process. The physical body is generally placed in an unconscious state for a very short time for the severing of the cord. Often one is simply placed in a deep sleep.

It has been predicted and documented that the new walk in souls come from a higher dimension with strong intentions to help raise the consciousness of the people on planet Earth. In doing so, humans become more caring of all life upon this planet.

These new souls have been considered high-minded souls, highly evolved souls, superior souls, superior beings etc. It is good that a transfer of egos are a part of this process. If the ego of the old soul remained, it would be difficult to be such an advanced being and not look at oneself as superior. Those who feel superior can never serve unconditionally. Every aspect of the human is considered prior to this amazing exchange. Walk ins can be found in all walks of life serving in many capacities. They may range from the most humbling lifestyles to the lifestyles of the rich and famous. Many humans have received a walk in soul and may never become aware that this process has occurred. Some only know that they have had a change in personality, lifestyle and other aspects of their being, even changes in relationships.   .

CHAPTER 8

MY PERSONAL
ACCOUNT OF
A WALK IN EXCHANGE

After days and nights in the nursing home having full-time care life had taken a drastic turn. I wasn't able to do anything for myself, being bedridden was a harrowing experience. Time stood still for me. I didn't do much thinking except the vague thought of being dead in a day or two. That thought being impressed upon me from a medical doctor. It seemed to be the dominant thought and it and had taken a hold on my mind.

On a particular night as I lay in my bed, my room seemed even darker than usual. As I laid motionless, sleep was evasive. I reflect upon the emptiness that had over taken me and the powerlessness that I had felt deep in my being. I felt like an empty vessel. A rag doll would have had more substance was my prevailing thought. I had lost my mobility therefore my time was spent simply lying in the bed. This particular day not only became life changing, it was life saving.

I began to drift off to sleep in the deep dark quiet of my room. Upon reflection the nursing home was unusually quiet and peaceful on this night. A serene energy seemed to permeate my room. Accustomed to hearing the small voice within, it was no surprise since when the inner dialogue began.

I heard a distinctive clear masculine voice firmly speak these words while instructing me   to "say the 23rd Psalm". Being in such a weakened state I attempted to ignore the voice, it would've taken too much strength to response or acknowledge the existence of the command. The voice was relentless, as I continued in my attempt to ignore it. Yet the voice would not be ignored. It became stronger and stronger until it seemed to have a distinct roar. It was compelling me to respond. Finally I was over powered by the persistence and strength of the voice. In a very weak voice I said "I already know the 23rd Psalm." As I was hoping that the voice would cease yet it continued with its request becoming stronger and stronger. Wishing the voice would come to an end I laid motionless in the bed. The voice seemed to be endless and wouldn't cease its powerful compelling voice. My only hope was to comply for I knew deeply that I would not be led astray. Where the physical was weak the spirit was strong.

I began to repeat the 23rd Psalm. With a slow drawl I began *the Lord is my shepherd I shall not want. He maketh me to lie down in green pastures he leadeth me beside the still waters He restoreth my soul. He leadeth in the paths of righteousness for his namesake. Yea though I walk through the valley of the shadow of death*....at that instant the clamor of an enormous great gong sounded off. As the sound resonated throughout my head, suddenly a vision in technicolor appeared as on a movie screen with the image of a great canyon with its deep valleys. An image was now before me of the most brilliant red and brown earth stately and massive. The voice came a second time. I lay in astonishment at the scenery of the the great beautiful canyon that had been presented to me. It roared again asking the question "how close are you to your shadow"? Somehow I knew the voice did not want an answer it wanted acknowledgement. I immediately envisioned my body and the shadow that a body creates. The voice then strongly stated "that's how close you are to death". At that moment the room seemed to transform into a color that was darker than midnight.

Immediately a figure appeared with an outlined form or shape of a human, yet not human. The figure was comprised of what appeared to be thousands of minute lights in many of the finest strands. I thought what a magnificent transparent being of light. As I lay in the bed in wonderment the light form approached my bed. An indescribable energy permeated the room and I felt it. I watched this form move ever so gracefully across the room. It seemed to be floating as I watched in wonder and amazement.

Somehow it effortlessly yet strategically contoured its form and placed itself on my solar plexus and stretched out into my body. At that point I drifted into a deep state of sleep and slept sound throughout the night.

Upon fully awakening the following day I distinctively recalled a very strange feeling and imagery in my mind. My mind replayed the nights events, and images as well as the sound of the voice like a video, over and over again. During my waking state the most strange occurrences were happening. As I sat up in the bed my head felt hollow but it had a brilliant bright light in it. How one can see a light within their own head I have no answer for, yet it was real for me. I still ponder and have questions regarding this particular light episode where I seemed to be able to scan my own inner body.

Staff in the nursing home were very cordial as I had developed a reasonable rapport. A nurse's assistant had come to do her daily rounds in my room. She happened to mention a circumstance that she had encountered and my immediate response was "let me shine light on the situation". I would begin to speak truth to her that seemed to astonish her. She begin to ask more questions and I would continue to say "let me shine some light on it". The assistant was very excited about what I will call a prophecy at this time. She hurried out of the room to share with a coworker the response that I had offered her. The same occurrence happened for her fellow employee. I remember, they had a strange look in their eyes as they observed me. I was still in a weakened state yet I felt strength rising up in me that I had not felt in a very, very long time.

The next day or so I began to improve dramatically. I was now able to stand on the side of the bed, which was a great improvement because I had not been able to walk. It was very difficult to walk but I had an unusually strong determination as I began to attempt to put my clothes on. This was a chore that I had not been able to perform. I started rehab with sweatpants. Simply having the ability to pick up one foot up and place it in the leg of those sweatpants did my heart well. I begin to progress at an accelerated rate, relevant to the condition I was in. In a short period of time, I was discharged an able to return home.

Abiding by the rules of the nursing home I had to be driven home in a van for the disabled. The experience and suffering as I traveled home is still etched in my memory. The normal screeching of brakes sent shock waves of pain through my body. How sound can affect a nervous system at a deep level was not within my scope of understanding. I had no clue as to the pain that I was to endure in the future due to the nerve sensitivity. The sensitivity of my nervous system on a scale from 1 to 10 was an easy 11. Over time I discovered that raindrops on the skin would feel like tiny darts being systematically thrown at me. How and why this occurred has never been medically explained. Today I believe it was the walk in soul adjusting to my nervous system. I have since learned that all humans have an electromagnetic field. My understanding is that the field of the original soul was interrupted, adjusted and even replaced. I am not sure if there is a medical explanation for these types of occurrences. Showers were difficult due to the excruciating pain. I was filled with skepticism of going outside of my home. I could not bear the pain from loud sounds, screeching tires, or any sudden noises. When it rained venturing outside was not even in the question.

It took several years for my body to adapt to the internal changes that caused nerve pain, and discomfort. Once the full exchange and acceptance is accomplished, a sense of normalcy and harmony can prevail. The light of the newly entered soul known as a walk-in had adapted to my physical body and we became more harmonious.

I had been dating a man for many years. He was very diligent with his support while I went through this dilemma. The very day that the nursing home delivered me to my house he came over. We had a significant relationship that seems that it would have stood the test of time, but something changed inside of me. I saw him as a stranger not from a physical point of view but from another place, an emotional place. Something had changed deep within me and I knew that I could no longer continue in the relationship.

He had done nothing wrong, nothing different than he had ever done but there was something in me that had very indifferent feelings towards him emotionally. In fact there was an emptiness, no emotions for him and all. It was the strangest thing - I never missed him. My sentiment was simply, I can't do this relationship anymore. I knew that it would be emotionally overwhelming for him, yet he felt like a stranger and it is not difficult to dismiss a stranger out of one's life.

Overtime I began to notice that I did not have the same emotional attachments to those that I had emotionally embraced prior to the walk in. I found myself simply tolerating friendships that in the past were deeply rooted had value and meaning. A detached feeling spilled over into blood relationships also.

One example was a friend that I felt more like a sister towards. We had been friends for over 25 years. One would think that a friendship of this nature would have lasted forever, yet it could not survive the new me. When friendships become generational, one would think that the ingredients for sustainability are present and held in love and affection. Yet I felt no real attachment. Not only did this happen in one friendship it happened in several. I never felt that it was a loss. I begin to pay more attention to myself and my detachment from old relationships. There was no emotional satisfaction in having a relationship with many people that I had in the past. It was easy to step away. I didn't realize at the time that my entire emotions had been altered. People places and things that had emotional value to me were very different now.

I found myself being drawn to people that saw life from a different perspective. I was attracted to people who embraced life and looked at the earth and all of the phenomena regarding the human in a different positive constructive way. I didn't realize the transformation in my relationships until

I dived deeply into self-awareness. As my awareness expanded I began to see myself from a different point of view.

My nervous system or maybe I should say my emotional body was very sensitive after the transformation of the new soul entering my physical body. My sensitivity would simply show up with the slightest infraction or the smallest hurt word. During that time I would have been considered to have thin skin. A person offended by the slightest infraction. I would find myself crying profusely in front of my perceived offender. This was extremely embarrassing to me as I was known to be a very strong assertive woman. It took a while for me to gain control of the excessive crying. As I look back I know that it stemmed from the sensitivity of my nervous system and emotional adjustments that had to take place.

The walk in soul had many adjustments to make. I have a firm belief that the new soul that walked into my body came from a place of higher dimensions where beings of light abide and had not encountered so much dark heavy energy and harshness that permeates areas of planet earth. When encountering harsh words or selfish deeds it was quite difficult for the new soul to handle. My physical body encasing the new soul was adjusting to the essence and energy of my new existence.

The new soul that walked into my physical body had to adapt to third dimensional norms in order to have harmony and balance in this dimension. Adjusting to selfishness, and greed has been a difficult task for the walk in soul in this physical body. The walk in soul had to adapt as well as understand my previous personality, nuances and style of communicating. These adjustments are very difficult and extremely taxing for both the receiver of the walk in soul and the new soul. Its was not an easy task for us.

Initially I felt as if I was looking out of the eyes of someone else. My awareness expanded as I began to see my fellow humans in a new and different way. As the adjustment continued my life began to change. There was a voice inside of me that was a very different voice and it was giving me directions and telling me to accomplish or conquer certain situations that were presented. I was receiving powerful information that was prophetic. I was certainly aided in conquering the emotions, utilizing strategies and words that were unfamiliar.

After being home for a while and bedridden, I was laying in my bed and I heard the voice clearly say "put on the gold high heel shoes" as the imagine of a specific pair of gold shoes lingered in my mind. I have always had a number of shoes that were the same color. As I lay in bed I laughed lightly at the idea. Me putting on high heel shoes just didn't make sense. The voice kept pressing me until I remember laying down the book that I was reading with my eyes now on my closet door, thinking of the whereabouts of the gold high heel shoes that I had been shown the image of. While looking at the closet I noticed several boxes of shoes sitting in the corner right next to the closet's door. I remember weighing the odds of me maneuvering from the bed to where the boxes of shoes were. I delayed for a while wondering if I had the energy or the mobility to move close enough towards the shoeboxes and not fall off the bed. I had to gauge my reach to keep myself balanced. After maneuvering across the bed I was able to knock the boxes over and grasp the box with the gold shoes in them. I utilized all my energy in accomplishing the task at hand.

Finally I was able to place both shoes on the bed with much effort. As I lay back on the bed to gain more energy my eyes were focused on the pair of gold shoes. I lay there wondering how foolish of me to attempt to put my feet in the shoes yet there was another aspect of me saying "it would be foolish for me not to try". After several minutes had past I decided to prop myself up on my pillows where I could really get a better look at the gold shoes. I came to the conclusion that after all the effort and energy that I had expended to get the shoes onto the bed, the least I could do was to attempt to try them on. I remember using my hand pulling my leg upward to gain access to my foot as I placed the high heel gold shoe on, then I placed the shoe on my other foot. At this point I was really exhausted. I laid straight back in the bed in order to regain my strength. As I lay back now I have full sight of my feet in the gold shoes. Of course I told myself that it be would ludicrous to attempt to stand up in these high heels. I laid there with the shoes on for quite a while as I hoped that something unusual would occur. Nothing happened. I looked at the shoes on my feet and I felt deep fear that if I attempted to stand in the shoes that I would fall.

Somehow a sense of confidence was overriding the fear and I felt an overwhelming desire to stand up. With much effort I cautiously sat on the side of the bed and placed both feet firmly on the floor while testing my body's balance. Finally I stood up weakly at first while attempting to stay balanced and keeping my hands touching the bed lightly. I took one step and then another and another, then I walked.

I couldn't believe that I was walking, without a walker, not holding on to the wall, yet balancing myself in high heel shoes. This was one of the days of my life that is etched in my memory. Thinking about it fills me with deep gratitude. As I sat down the voice of the neurologist echoed in my mind "you will never walk again".

I remember feeling that my life had taken a turn for the good. The emotion that I felt on that day sprung up as joy and hope throughout my be-ing. Oh what a glorious day. My physical body had many adjustments to make as they are still ongoing. I think improvements will be made forever.

Not only does the walk in effect the physicality it also affects the men-tal aspect of a human. It affected me in many ways. After the first year the adjustment was mentally draining. Disoriented seems to describe the state that I was in. I have shared that my walking was not stable but there was no stability in any aspect of my being.

Many times in communicating I would simply be at a loss of words to describe a person, place or event. Communicating in the fashion that I was accustomed to was non existent. My nonverbal communications were all over the place, sending distorted messages. My eye contact was not my norm. My eyes were not focused in a timely fashion which assisted in throwing all of my non verbals off kilter. With unstable walking, unfocused eye contact, and a loss of words caused a deep sadness inside. I was a basket case.

I remember going to a car dealer and seeking out a salesman whom I was familiar with and had purchased two cars from before. Upon greeting me he asked "are you drunk"? I remember standing there feeling shame and embarrassment since I could not offer an intelligent response. This was very disheartening for me for I prided myself that I didn't drink or do drugs or ingest anything that was not good for my body prior to the diagnosis as well as after. His statement hit me below the belt. I was not aware that I had been viewed in such a manner. Yet the salesman only responded to what he saw. It seemed as if it took me forever to offer a respond by finally saying "I don't even drink wine". There were more embarrassing moments during the adjustment that my body was going through. My emotions were rampant from highs to lows. I was extremely sensitive to how I was spoken to and more sensitive to how I was treated. It was an emotionally painful time.

Most aspects of who I was changed and shifted. I no longer had an interest in things that interested me prior to the walk in soul. I recall becoming more tolerant of the flaws and shortcomings of others. I had gained a new outlook on life. Life was different for me in many ways . Simply, I had changed. I looked at humans through a different lens.

I recall while in the nursing home I spoke with friends and we still maintain a close relationship. The couple both hold PhD's. I had been friends with the husband and the wife team long before they were married. I spoke with the husband who is a researcher on religion and cultures. Since we often engaged in conversations regarding different phenomena that are not widely known or practiced. He was also a trusted confidant. I felt an urge to tell him what had happened on the unusual night when I was awakened by a voice directing me to say Psalm 23.

He listened patiently to my vivid description of this occurrence and immediately respond that I had been given a new soul. I asked questions regarding his statement of the new soul and he provided answers. He claimed that ancient text had alluded to this type of occurrence. He then firmly stated that is what had happened to me. Years after, even today as we still engage in conversations, he reminds me that I have a new soul and

I am not the age that our biological bodies generally indicates. He claims that I should count my age starting at the time that the new soul came into my body. He has constantly reminded me that I have been given a second chance on life with a brand-new soul.

Although he reminded me for many years of this new soul exchange, I took it quite lightly. It was as if the new soul wanted to be shielded, and did not want attention or to be identified as being new or different . We wanted to remain a secret. Fear of being under attack verbally or ridiculed seemed to be my rational for not exposing my walk in soul exchange.

CHAPTER 9

BARING MY SOULS TRUTH

While reading a community spiritual magazine I came across an advertisement that described several organizations and groups that met to enhance or empower themselves spiritually. My attention was attracted to a specific group and my interest peaked. Soon after I went online to look at the website.

There were many groups and a variety of interesting topics were highlighted. A particular group attracted my attention as I was compelled to read all of the information that was provided. It was located a distance from my home yet it wasn't too far to travel. In order to participate in the group session a questionnaire had to be filled out online. Again this is something that I generally would never do. I was not comfortable in giving out personal information online. I decided to look at the profiles of others before completing my own profile. It then dawned on me that I would be entering a group of people who were spiritually inclined and yet strangers. I toyed around with the idea for a while as I was being inspired to move forward and join the group.

The name of the non-for-profit organization was The Gathering Lighthouse. I really liked the name it sounded so welcoming as well as spiritual. Although a variety of locations were available, I was still hesitant in regards to the group. I didn't know it's belief system, as well as how the group would respond to me.

The group met once a week and I finally complied with the groups requirement. I asked a friend to fill out her profile that she would be able to accompany me to the first meeting. At each group meeting I found that it was customary to give an overview as to your purpose for wanting to join such a group. We also would share any gifts or special talents that one may posses that was rooted in the spirit world or any unusual phenomena. After meeting the group's hostess an other participants I felt very comfortable with my interaction with them. I continued to participate in the weekly meetings. I became more trusting of the confidentiality of the group. Each member of the group was very open as each gave an overview or a summary of their particular interest or special spiritual abilities, such as clairvoyance, telepathic abilities, etc. I finally opened up and shared with the group that I had a near death experience and was privileged to a walk in soul that had given me new life. I didn't feel judged at all, in fact I was embraced more than ever.

After participating in the group I became more comfortable exposing the intimate details regarding my walk in soul experience. The leader of the local group where I attended asked if she could speak with me personally at the end of the meeting. I immediately agreed to meet with her. It was mandatory for the participants to sign a written acknowledgement that we individually would never divulge information relevant to other participants.

We would adhere to confidentiality. I waited patiently as each participant left the meeting room wondering what the nature of our conversation would be. The woman whose name was Renee Oswald asked for permission to share my walk-in soul experience with the Organizations founder. I gave my consent for her to do so.

At the meeting the following week, Renee informed me that the founder of The Gathering Lighthouse wanted to know if I would be willing to provide a workshop regarding the walk in soul. I agreed to do so.

At the time I had not considered the time that would be necessary for me to reflect back and recapture details that I had simply not visited over a long period of time. I had to organize my experiences in a chronological organized order as to present the facts as they occurred. Reflecting back upon all the details brought up many emotions that I had stored deeply within me. I was blindsided by the intensity of the feelings that I had to re-visit. The day came quickly that I was to do the presentation.

As I arrived at the center where I would be the guest speaker, I began to feel a sense of relief and freedom as I had hidden my truth from myself as well as others. I was to provided a two hour presentation to this non for profit organization. This is a center where profound spiritual information is disseminated. This is a place where individuals would find like minded people seeking to expand their knowledge regarding spiritual topics and unusual phenomena while most embodied a variety of spiritual gifts.

I was introduced by the head Founder and Executive Director June May Kortum who is a well know medium. The time had finally come and Renee Oswald began her introduction of me. I was quite surprised to hear her speak such wonderful words in regards to me.

I began to walk towards the podium. Those in attendance seemed to look through to my soul and I'm certain that many were capable due to their gifted abilities. The energy was intense, filled with anticipation as I am now in the main headquarters where the majority of people I did not know. I remember thinking, "I am in the presence of mediums and others who had what I will call second sight".

As I was approximately five feet from the podium a woman sitting very close to where I was to speak gently touched me. I stopped to hear what was so pressing that she needed to say. With a firm tone the red headed woman distinguished looking curtly stated " I've been studying walk in souls for many, many years."

In that moment she gave me a look that indicated that, you had better know what you're talking about because I'm well versed in this matter. Graciously I thanked her and stepped up to begin the public exposure of who I AM, as I thought how risky this must be. What would those in the audience think of me now that I have revealed the most personal aspects of my journey with a soul exchange.

My presentation went quite well as I was able to articulate the walk in soul experience in detail. Waves of energy flowed throughout the room filled with compassion. I felt a peaceful energy permeating all around me.

There was a question and answer session where I was asked to go into more details in regards to the walk in soul. I could feel the positive loving energy filling the room. When the Q & A ended, I was very surprised that a line had formed where participants simply wanted to hug me and some begin to cry.

This was an overwhelming experience for me. In that moment I thought about individuals who have lived hidden lives must feel a great sense of freedom and love once accepted for their true authentic self. The once sceptic red head woman hugged me and confirmed that she new that I was a walk in and that she had never heard such an informed and detailed account as I had given.

The woman whose name is Deb Freuh has a large following that participates in her organization, The Worldwide Metaphysical Tribe. She and I have developed a mutual respect for the innate skills that we embody. As she bears profound gifts we have a deep friendship. Overtime this same woman informed me of a book that was written several decades earlier regarding walk ins.

I had never seen anything regarding a walk in soul in the written word. I had only casually mentioned the walk in phenomena to a very few people outside of my spiritual group. I finally received the recommended book as it was difficult to get and seemed to be out of print. It was quite descriptive as it peeled back and laid bare who I was. It adequately described many of my experiences regarding the walk in soul from inception to the many new skills that the walk in soul embodies.

The idea that the groundwork had been laid prior to my exchange was very exciting. The idea that I had tangible evidence written by a well respected, revered author was even more intriguing.

Reading about a new soul and soul exchange using the name walk in adequately describing this unusual phenomena was so amazing to me. I felt like a lost person finally being found. I began to talk to those who I considered evolved spiritual friends and shared many aspects of me that they had not known. I was so excited to know that there was a name attached to my experience that was documented by another soul. I had only known one person who was able to identify me as having a walk in soul.

Acceptance and acknowledgment of my existence as a walk in soul gave me a renewed confidence. I felt as if I had been hiding in the shadows and now I could come out into the light, because it confirmed that others new that I existed. It was a great feeling.

The new insight in regards to the term walk in soul gleaned from the newly referred book infused me with joy, anticipation, and wonderment. As I read the signs and symptoms of a walk in that was written well before my experience, it assisted me profoundly in my liberation.

I began to contemplate the illness, the nursing home event and many other events that led me to where I am today. I was able to connect all the dots and all the circumstances that had occurred in my life. I now had a clear understanding of the new direction that my life had taken as well as the possibilities.

Gratitude for the walk in soul was my inner mantra. My life had seemed to take on a deeper purpose and meaning, but I had not connected on the inner with the new soul that came here and used my body to help planet earth heal and move forward.

After reflection and contemplation, I clearly understood that I could have been dead if not for the blessing of the walk in soul. My inner sight became more expansive as I related to my walk in soul and the value that it brought to my spiritual development.

Approximately a year later I was requested to provide a second presentation regarding the walk in soul in a northwestern suburban area of Chicago, Illinois. Providing my first presentation was somewhat of a coming out event. It offered a sense of mental freedom as I had held the idea of me being a walk in very close with the thought to never expose myself.

Now I had committed to expose myself on a deeper level, because I had grown into more knowledge of who and what my truth was. The time was fast approaching the day for me to speak. I thought it would be wise to dig up the old notes that I had utilized in regards to my first speech on the walk in. I had developed a set of notes to keep me focused in an orderly fashion during the speaking engagement. I have always been one who maintained documents for everything. Locating the notes that I felt were necessary for me to stay focused was not an easy chore. After locating the notes, I strategically placed them on my dining room table in plain sight, as a reminder that I must review them on the next day. I went to sleep that night with the idea of adding events that had occurred over the past year.

Upon awakening I went about my morning with my everyday ritual, shower, making a pot of coffee and then meditation. I then began shuffling the papers that held my notes. While inserting and adding new information a strange feeling swept over me rapidly compelling me into the deepest state of sadness than I have ever known.

I immediately wrapped my arms around myself as if giving myself a needed hug. While holding tight to my middle section, my solar plexus area while a deep primal cry poured forth from my being that jerked my body as if in waves. The penetrating sounds of such an uncontrollable nature that I had never experienced before poured profusely from a deep place within me. The crying was so deep it felt as if it would never cease.

I struggled to lift myself from the chair, enter a bedroom and throw myself on the bed where the crying continued for a period of time as my body racked with deep intense sadness and emotional pain. While seeking to recover from the overwhelming feeling of despair, a deep knowing came over me.

I was grieving the old soul that had left and made room for the new soul. I understood this truth, yet I had never considered it before. The idea that one would grieve such a lost had never crossed my mind. Finally I gathered myself and washed my tear streaked face. Shortly after I took my seat at the table again to continue reviewing my notes I felt a new lightness within me as if something had ben lifted off of me.

After a period of time of maybe a year or more, I began to really think about my inner self and the soul. As I did the thought came that I had never really embraced the new soul or offered any appreciation for providing me with a new opportunity at life. I thought how selfish of me not to view my soul and the exchange in gracefulness and gratitude. I began to look in my mirror daily, deep into my own eyes and say I love you, referring to my soul. This process assisted me in seeing my life as more valuable than ever before. On all levels harmony prevailed. Peace began to permeate my entire being and I felt whole.

I begin to pay more attention to myself and my spiritual side. In contemplation I learned more about the walk in soul, it's relationship to me in the physical as well as the spiritual. It also began to reveal more of itself to me. In the silence it was explained how I had become more compassionate and sympathetic, while a strong desire was infused in me to serve the planet and all who dwell within. I found myself being thrust into global organizations that were designed to assist humanity. I was sincerely concerned and deeply touched by the suffering of those on planet earth.

Now I was in a position to assist humanity in a number of ways. Many synchronicities were occurring, placing me where I needed to be at a given time to do humanitarian work. I found many patterns in my life where the hand of the divine was working. I understood that the new walk in soul needed a lengthy amount of time to finished the work of the old soul that it could now step up its pace in doing the work that it had come to do.

The walk in soul carries many gifts or variables that I did not have with my departed soul. There are many skills that come with such an advanced soul. I now had visions where I have seen all manners of events that were to be futuristic. I have seen scenarios being played out that describes futuristic happenings sometimes in the personal lives of another or on a global scale. Many times I have a knowing about people places and things prior to it's happenings. Often times I can speak the words that a person is about to speak and I can finish their sentences. Sometimes I know the demeanor or attitude of a stranger prior to an introduction. I receive information from the Ascended Masters. Information is channeled to me that predicts futuristic happenings, information about the galaxies or solutions to problems that humans incur. While asleep information feels like it is been downloaded and I wake up with knowledge that I had no prior understanding of. I have an unusual ability to write poetry especially prose that is so profound, when read publicly people become teary-eyed. I have had the opportunity to be a vessel for healing others. I am constantly discovering gifts that come from the walk in soul. I can discern sincerity immediately in a person. Sometimes while taking a nap I am told of a particular herb or supplement that a specific person needs to become whole.

The ability to manifest is a beautiful gift that I inherited with the walk in soul. The ability to think or visualize a thing often will come to pass very quickly. I am constantly being informed and directed as to where to go and what to do. It is always for the highest good of all involved. Often I am giving information that needs to be disseminated to large groups of people, and I follow the instructions.

I have been awakened at 3 o'clock or 4 o'clock am, very early in the morning with information being poured into me and I have been told where it should be disseminated. Often information is directed for me to share with certain individuals. Many times I am told that the information must be diluted that it can be digested by those who need more spiritual growth. Much information is channeled and I write and journal often. The information has such deep meaning that I often revisit the information and gain deeper insight. I have been informed, inspired and motivated through these writings that flow from my most inner self.

My life's path has been laid out in front of me, as I have been directed to assist and help humanity in a number of ways. This ranges from simply being available, that my inner light energy may radiate outward to raise the vibration of others, to more complex directives that enable me to touch the inner essence of other groups of humans. I have been privy to knowledge that allows me to communicate through heart energy as well as a broader understanding of the energy and power of light.

I have had the ability to communicate with loved ones that have passed on. Clear messages have been disseminated to me from many of those who have made their transition. These messages sometimes are meant to be forwarded to loved ones who were left behind suffering their loss.

Galactic information has been a privilege for me to have a deeper insight on how planet earth fits into the galactic formation and it's importance in regards to other planetary systems. Those who are aware of UFOs and the extraterrestrial presences can relate to this phenomena as humans on earth are contacted and communicated with, often through telepathic means. I have had this experience also. I will not put a limitation up on the walk in soul because I have no idea of its possibilities. It would be foolish of me to believe that my knowledge is all that exists.

As I stated earlier I have a deep feeling that the walk-in soul had no desire to reveal itself to the public. After being introduced to the walk in term, a chain of events began to unfold. I believe that the walk in soul set the circumstances into play, since a walk in embodies attributes that are expansive. My understanding and awareness grew regarding this new soul. I simply begin to have an understanding that was not rooted in what is considered normal or natural forms of learning.

108

A level of appreciation flourished in me more than ever at the thought that I had been given a second chance at life. A second chance at life causes one to think in ways that compels them to look at life from a deeper perspective and a deeper appreciation. I began to marvel at the changes and newfound abilities that I was discovering. A genuine self-love was a new idea that I embraced especially from the soul aspect. My self-esteem grew by leaps and bounds, as I recognized and identified myself with the walk-in soul. Since there is an exchange of egos, it keeps walk ins balanced and in a position to serve. Ultimately that is the goal.

I found a new connection with nature. The oceans, the trees, plant life and all lifeforms felt as if I had a deep connection. The depth of the emotional attachment of all living things seemed to come alive within me. A deep love and concern for the planet earth became my focus.

There are those that believe that there are no accidents in life. Synchronicity became my way of viewing life, where simultaneous events began to appear. I began to look at life as a chain with many links. I was able to look back and reflect upon an event that would cause a chain of events to occur. Being able to connect past events with present events gave me insight into future events. At this point I can began to expect certain outcomes. This is a component of manifesting. I knew that the walk in soul was preparing me for work on a planetary level. I believe that it had to awaken in me a love for planetary life and then place me solidly in a place to affect issues that plague the planet.

I had never been one who was keen on the idea of volunteering. It just so happened that while under a professional contractual agreement, a gentleman asked me to join a global humanitarian organization. Initially I was hoping that he would cease asking me to join the organization. I wanted as much free time to and for myself that was available. I could not see myself donating time. Time was a precious commodity. I felt that my life was already filled with enough to do. This gentleman would not cease asking me to come to a meeting with his organization.

After I used up all of my excuses, I decide to attend a meeting. I continued to join the meetings and before I was aware I had become intricately involved physically as well as emotionally. After being involved in this organization for a few years other circumstances began to unfold that would establish me even more deeply into this well known credible organization.

The organization was a catalyst that placed me in several other global organizations, whose goals are to raise the quality of life of humans across this planet. I also found myself helping a great number of individuals as a spiritual counselor. Soul satisfaction is always the outcome for me.

My desire is to assist in freeing walk in souls who are everywhere, many unknowing of this life saving exchange. They need to be legitimized, as many have never heard of the term walk in. Walk ins possess the qualities to assist the planet as evolution is continuously in motion. Every life force on planet earth is marching forward towards higher aspects of itself. Walk in souls are here to assist humanity in the process of growth, evolution and transformation. Transitioning into a new state of being can be troubling to the mind, body and spirit. We the walk ins come with the skills and compassion for this highly ordered task. Many are not aware of their purpose. Some feel powerless and alone in going through the transition of becoming a walk in soul. I am and will be bringing into the light more information of the walk in phenomena that the populous will have more information and develop compassion and respect for these fortunate humans who embody not only a new soul but a spirit from higher dimensions that has come to assist planet earth.

As we bypass the common birthing process walk in souls are ready to get into the thick of things. The goal is to help this planet move into a golden age where peace and harmony will prevail. We are working to save the mineral kingdom, the plant kingdom the beautiful waterways as well as the human kingdom. All that reside on planet earth will benefit from the beings called walk in souls in one way or another. A programmed mind cannot phantom the idea of a walk in soul, but I guarantee the effects of these beings on this planet will last infinitely.

While in years to come future generations will pay homage to these selfless beings as they carry profound light into the darkest places on this planet. There are certain characteristics that are unique to a walk in exchange. You may be one. These powerful light workers are seen and unseen pushing humanity forward out of the darkness of third dimensional realities and into a higher consciousness, where humans will gain an in-depth understanding that we are more than what we have been told. If you are reading this book, it is not by accident. This book is comprised of spiritual energy, for the words come from a different place. You have embodied these words and they will raise your awareness and free you to see everything from a deeper place. A place infused with deep light as you are but are yet to be told.

Made in the USA
Monee, IL
18 March 2023

29618985R00080